THE BOOK OF POETRY

BRITISH POETS
PAGES 1883-2216

THE BOOK OF POETRY

Collected from the Whole Field
of British and American Poetry.
Also Translations of Important
Poems from Foreign Languages.

Selected and Annotated
with an Introduction by
EDWIN MARKHAM

Poetry fettered,
fetters the human race.
—William Blake.

VOLUME VII

WM. H. WISE & CO.
NEW YORK   1927

CONTENTS

vii

ix

BRITISH POETS

From 1811
To 1830

WILLIAM MAKEPEACE THACKERAY
ENGLAND, 1811—1863

THACKERAY carried deep personal sorrows to the grave;
and in his *End of the Play* he touches upon the
anxious questions of the meaning of life's disasters. He
felt the difficulty of justifying "the ways of God to men."
He thinks that we confront an "immutable design", and
that we must "bow before the awful will." I feel that
our disasters are due—not to "the awful will" of Heaven,
but are due to the failure of men to organize God's providence on earth, their failure to build a brotherly order as
a shelter over the people.

From "The Age of Wisdom"

HO, pretty page, with the dimpled chin,
    That never has known the barber's shear,
All your wish is woman to win,
This is the way that boys begin—
    Wait till you come to Forty Year.

Curly gold locks cover foolish brains,
    Billing and cooing is all your cheer;
Sighing and singing of midnight strains,
Under Bonnybell's window panes—
    Wait till you come to Forty Year.

Forty times over let Michaelmas pass,
    Grizzling hair the brain doth clear—
Then you know a boy is an ass,
Then you know the worth of a lass,
    Once you have come to Forty Year. . . .

1883

Gillian's dead, God rest her bier,
　How I loved her twenty years syne!
Marian's married, but I sit here
Alone and merry at Forty Year,
　Dipping my nose in the Gascon wine.

At the Church Gate

ALTHOUGH I enter not,
　Yet round about the spot
　　Ofttimes I hover;
And near the sacred gate,
With longing eyes I wait,
　Expectant of her.

The minster bell tolls out
Above the city's rout
　And noise and humming:
They've hushed the minster bell;
The organ 'gins to swell—
　She's coming, coming!

My lady comes at last,
Timid and stepping fast,
　And hastening hither,
With modest eyes downcast:
She comes—she's here—she's past!
　May Heaven go with her!

Kneel undisturbed, fair saint!
Pour out your praise or plaint
　Meekly and duly:

1884

I will not enter there,
To sully your pure prayer
      With thoughts unruly.

But suffer me to pace
Round the forbidden place,
      Lingering a minute,
Like outcast spirits, who wait,
And see, through Heaven's gate,
      Angels within it.

The Sorrows of Werther

WERTHER had a love for Charlotte
      Such as words could never utter:
Would you know how first he met her?
      She was cutting Bread-and-Butter.

Charlotte was a married lady,
      And a moral man was Werther;
And, for all the wealth of Indies,
      Would do nothing for to hurt her.

So he sighed and pined and ogled,
      And his passion boiled and bubbled;
Till he blew his silly brains out,
      And no more was by it troubled.

Charlotte, having seen his body
      Borne before her on a shutter,
Like a well-conducted person,
      Went on cutting Bread-and-Butter.

1885

WILLIAM MAKEPEACE THACKERAY

The Noble Art of Murdering

LAST year, my Love, it was my hap
    Behind a grenadier to be;
And, but he wore a hairy cap,
    No taller man, methinks, than me.

Prince Albert and the Queen, God wot
    (Be blessings on the glorious pair!)
Before us passed. I saw them not—
    I only saw a cap of hair.

Your orthodox historian puts
    In foremost rank the soldier thus,
The red-coat bully in his boots,
    That hides the march of men from us.

He puts him there in foremost rank,
    You wonder at his cap of hair:
You hear his sabre's cursèd clank,
    His spurs are jingling everywhere.

Go to! I hate him and his trade:
    Who bade us so to cringe and bend,
And all God's peaceful people made
    To such as him subservient?

Tell me what find we to admire
    In epaulets and scarlet coats—
In men, because they load and fire,
    And know the art of cutting throats?

1886

WILLIAM MAKEPEACE THACKERAY

From "The End of the Play"

THE play is done; the curtain drops,
   Slow falling, to the prompter's bell:
A moment yet the actor stops,
And looks around, to say farewell.
It is an irksome word and task;
And, when he's laughed and said his say,
He shows, as he removes the mask,
A face that's anything but gay.

One word, ere yet the evening ends,
Let's close it with a parting rhyme,
And pledge a hand to all young friends,
As fits the merry Christmas-time.
On life's wide scene you, too, have parts,
That Fate ere long shall bid you play;
Good night! with honest gentle hearts
A kindly greeting go alway!

Come wealth or want, come good or ill,
Let young and old accept their part,
And bow before the Awful Will,
And bear it with an honest heart,
Who misses, or who wins the prize.
Go, lose or conquer as you can;
But if you fail, or if you rise,
Be each, pray God, a gentleman.

1887

ALFRED DOMETT
ENGLAND, 1811—1887

IT is to this English poet and colonial statesman that Robert Browning refers in *Waring* and *The Guardian Angel*. The two poets were intimate friends. In 1842 Domett went to New Zealand, where he held many public offices; and in 1871 he returned to England, where he died.

A Christmas Hymn

IT was the calm and silent night!
   Seven hundred years and fifty-three
Had Rome been growing up to might,
   And now was queen of land and sea.
No sound was heard of clashing wars—
   Peace brooded o'er the hushed domain:
Apollo, Pallas, Jove and Mars
     Held undisturbed their ancient reign,
       In the solemn midnight,
         Centuries ago.

'Twas in the calm and silent night!
   The Senator of haughty Rome
Impatient urged his chariot's flight,
   From lordly revel rolling home:
Triumphal arches, gleaming, swell
   His breast with thoughts of boundless sway:
What recked the Roman what befell
   A paltry province far away,

1888

ALFRED DOMETT

In the solemn midnight,
Centuries ago?

Within that province far away
  Went plodding home a weary boor;
A streak of light before him lay,
  Fallen through a half-shut stable door
Across his path. He passed—for naught
  Told what was going on within:
How keen the stars, his only thought—
  The air how calm, and cold, and thin,
    In the solemn midnight,
      Centuries ago!

Oh, strange indifference! low and high
  Drowsed over common joys and cares;
The earth was still—but knew not why;
  The world was listening, unawares—
How calm a moment may precede
  One that shall thrill the world forever!
To that still moment, none would heed,
  Man's doom was linked no more to sever—
    In the solemn midnight,
      Centuries ago!

It is the calm and solemn night!
  A thousand bells ring out and throw
Their joyous peals abroad and smite
  The darkness—charmed and holy now!
The night that erst no name had worn,
  To it a happy name is given;
For in that stable lay, new-born,
  The peaceful Prince of Earth and Heaven,
    In the solemn midnight,
      Centuries ago!

1889

ROBERT BROWNING
ENGLAND, 1812—1889

Browning's father was a clerk in the Bank of England, a man highly appreciative of art and literature. Young Browning was educated chiefly at home in his father's library, where he devoured the older poets. He began early to write. His first poem, *Pauline,* was completed before he was twenty. It foreshadowed his later *Paracelsus* and *Sordello,* each also being a study of a soul.

In the early forties, many of his best poems appeared in the volume *Bells and Pomegranates.* In this period he married most romantically the great woman poet, Elizabeth Barrett. They spent fifteen rich, fruitful years together in Italy, where she died. In this period, Browning created the dramatic monologue.

The Ring and the Book, in which the same story is told from many points of view, is a poem of original perception, laboriously long, yet lit with dramatic passages and sprinkled with splendid lines. His later poems keep all his old fire, as is shown by *Asolando,* written after he was seventy-five.

Browning, because of obscurities of style, was a long time gaining an audience. Like Tennyson's, although vastly different in technique, his work was pregnant with the scientific and spiritual problems of his time. Browning saw things moving from a center of human feeling and passion; Tennyson saw things circling about the pivot of law.

The processes of Browning's mind were swift, leaping over gaps and obstructions, running far ahead of the steps of his readers. His allusions, often covering esoteric and remote fields of knowledge, often uttered with subtle and cryptic compression and frequent defiance of syntax—

these allusions tended to bewilder the plodding Victorian. Browning is not often to be read as one runs: he must be read more than once with the mind stretched to full tension. But, sweeping in as they do every province of art, literature, and science, his pages yield many riches.

Invincible optimism, the belief that all is going well and ever tending onward and upward, is one of the constant factors in Browning's work. His wholesale optimism is irritating to many who see the hopeless devastations going on in this mortal struggle. He is a thorough individualist. He does not seem to realize that men must band together in a divine brotherhood to make possible the Providence that will shelter the race and open the gates of opportunity to every son of man.

Browning, however enigmatic, has the power at times to speak magnificently and significantly from the heart. Although a philosopher and a psychologist, yet he is the supreme poet of love in our era; and perhaps no one equals him—at his highest—in the power of shining, stabbing phrase, in the flash of vital dialogue, in the probe of revealing soliloquy, in thrust and parry of dramatic encounters.

Browning surpasses all other poets (Shakespeare excepted) in his power to throw light upon the difficult and anxious questions that besiege the soul of man.

You'll Love Me Yet

FROM "PIPPA PASSES"

YOU'LL love me yet!—and I can tarry
   Your love's protracted growing:
June reared that bunch of flowers you carry,
   From seeds of April's sowing.

1891

I plant a heartful now: some seed
    At least is sure to strike,
And yield—what you'll not pluck indeed,
    Not love, but, may be, like.

You'll look at least on love's remains,
    A grave's one violet:
Your look?—that pays a thousand pains.
    What's death? You'll love me yet!

New Year's Hymn

FROM "PIPPA PASSES"

ALL service ranks the same with God:
    If now, as formerly he trod
Paradise, his presence fills
Our earth, each only as God wills
Can work—God's puppets, best and worst,
Are we; there is no last nor first.

Say not "a small event!" Why "small?"
Costs it more pain that this, ye call
A "great event," should come to pass,
Than that? Untwine me from the mass
Of deeds which make up life, one deed
Power shall fall short in or exceed!

1892

ROBERT BROWNING

Ottima and Sebald, Two Lovers
FROM "PIPPA PASSES"

*Before I present Pippa's famous song, it seems only fair to
give the portion of introductory dialogue between Ottima,
wife of Luca, and her lover Sebald, the two having just
murdered her husband. Browning is said to have been
walking alone through an English woodland when the
image flashed upon him of some one passing thus alone
through life; one apparently too obscure to leave a trace of
his or her passage, yet exercising a lasting though uncon-
scious influence at every step of it; and the image shaped
itself into Felippa or Pippa, the little silk-mill-worker of
Asolo.*

OTTIMA. Buried in woods we lay, you recollect;
　　Swift ran the searching tempest overhead;
And ever and anon some bright white shaft
Burned through the pine-tree roof, here burned and
　　　　there,
As if God's messenger through the close wood screen
Plunged and replunged his weapon at a venture,
Feeling for guilty thee and me: then broke
The thunder like a whole sea overhead—
　　Sebald. Yes!
　　Ottima. —While I stretched myself upon you, hands
To hands, my mouth to your hot mouth, and shook
All my locks loose, and covered you with them—
You, Sebald, the same you!
　　Sebald.　　　　　　Slower, Ottima!
　　Ottima. And as we lay—
　　Sebald.　　　　　　Less vehemently! Love me!
Forgive me! Take not words, mere words, to heart!

1893

Your breath is worse than wine.   Breathe slow, speak
    slow!
Do not lean on me!
  Ottima.   Sebald, as we lay,
Rising and falling only with our pants,
Who said, "Let death come now!   'Tis right to die!
Right to be punished!   Naught completes such bliss
But woe!"   Who said that?
  Sebald.   How did we ever rise?
Was't that we slept?   Why did it end?
  Ottima.   I felt you
Taper into a point the ruffled ends
Of my loose locks 'twixt both your humid lips,
My hair is fallen now: knot it again!
  Sebald.   I kiss you now, dear Ottima, now and now!
This way?   Will you forgive me—be once more
My great queen?
  Ottima.   Bind it thrice about my brow;
Crown me your queen, your spirit's arbitress,
Magnificent in sin.   Say that!
  Sebald.   I crown you
My great white queen, my spirit's arbitress,
Magnificent . . .
    [*From without is heard the voice of* PIPPA *singing—*

> *The year's at the spring*
> *And day's at the morn;*
> *Morning's at seven;*
> *The hillside's dew-pearled;*
> *The lark's on the wing;*
> *The snail's on the thorn:*
> *God's in his heaven—*
> *All's right with the world!*

                      [PIPPA *passes.*

1894

My Star

ALL that I know
　　Of a certain star
Is, it can throw
　　(Like the angled spar)
Now a dart of red,
　　Now a dart of blue;
Till my friends have said
　　They would fain see, too,
My star that dartles the red and the blue!
Then it stops like a bird; like a flower, hangs furled:
　　They must solace themselves with the Saturn above it,
What matter to me if their star is a world?
　　Mine has opened its soul to me; therefore I love it.

Meeting at Night

*Here is one of the immortal things—not a word too many,
not a word too few. It is a lyric round and perfect as a
star.*

THE gray sea and the long black land;
　　And the yellow half-moon large and low;
And the startled little waves that leap
In fiery ringlets from their sleep,
As I gain the cove with pushing prow,
And quench its speed i' the slushy sand.

Then a mile of warm sea-scented beach;
Three fields to cross till a farm appears;
A tap at the pane, the quick sharp scratch

And blue spurt of a lighted match,
And a voice less loud, through its joys and fears,
Than the two hearts beating each to each!

Parting at Morning

ROUND the cape of a sudden came the sea,
  And the sun looked over the mountain's rim:
And straight was a path of gold for him,
And the need of a world of men for me.

The Last Ride Together

I SAID—Then, dearest, since 'tis so,
  Since now at length my fate I know,
Since nothing all my love avails,
Since all my life seemed meant for fails,
  Since this was written and needs must be—
My whole heart rises up to bless
Your name in pride and thankfulness!
Take back the hope you gave—I claim
Only a memory of the same;
And this beside, if you will not blame—
  Your leave for one more last ride with me.

My mistress bent that brow of hers,
Those deep dark eyes where pride demurs
When pity would be softening through,
Fixed me a breathing-while or two
  With life or death in the balance: right!

1896

The blood replenished me again;
My last thought was at least not vain:
I and my mistress, side by side
Shall be together, breathe and ride,
So, one day more am I deified.
  Who knows but the world may end to-night?

Hush! if you saw some western cloud
All billowy-bosomed, over-bowed
By many benedictions—sun's
And moon's and evening-star's at once—
  And so, you, looking and loving best,
Conscious grew, your passion drew
Cloud, sunset, moonrise, star-shine too,
Down on you, near and yet more near,
Till flesh must fade for heaven was here!—
Thus leant she and lingered—joy and fear!
  Thus lay she a moment on my breast.

Then we began to ride. My soul
Smoothed itself out, a long-cramped scroll
Freshening and fluttering in the wind.
Past hopes already lay behind.
  What need to strive with a life awry?
Had I said that, had I done this,
So might I gain, so might I miss.
Might she have loved me? just as well
She might have hated, who can tell!
Where had I been now if the worst befell?
  And here we are riding, she and I.

Fail I alone, in words and deeds?
Why, all men strive and who succeeds?
We rode; it seemed my spirit flew,

Saw other regions, cities new,
  As the world rushed by on either side.
I thought—All labor, yet no less
Bear up beneath their unsuccess.
Look at the end of work, contrast
The petty done, the undone vast,
This present of theirs with the hopeful past!
  I hoped she would love me; here we ride.

What hand and brain went ever pained?
What heart alike conceived and dared?
What act proved all its thought had been?
What will but felt the fleshly screen?
  We ride and I see her bosom heave.
There's many a crown for who can reach.
Ten lines, a statesman's life in each!
The flag stuck on a heap of bones,
A soldier's doing! what atones?
They scratch his name on the Abbey-stones.
  My riding is better, by their leave.

What does it all mean, poet? Well,
Your brains beat into rhythm, you tell
What we felt only; you expressed
You hold things beautiful the best,
  And pace them in rhyme so, side by side.
'Tis something, nay 'tis much: but then,
Have you yourself what's best for men?
Are you—poor, sick, old ere your time—
Nearer one whit your own sublime
Than we who never have turned a rhyme?
  Sing, riding's a joy! For me, I ride.

And you, great sculptor—so, you gave
A score of years to Art, her slave,

1898

And that's your Venus, whence we turn
To yonder girl that fords the burn!
  You acquiesce, and shall I repine?
What, man of music, you grown gray
With notes and nothing else to say,
Is this your sole praise from a friend,
"Greatly his opera's strains intend,
But in music we know how fashions end!"
  I gave my youth: but we ride, in fine.

Who knows what's fit for us? Had fate
Proposed bliss here should sublimate
My being—had I signed the bond—
Still one must lead some life beyond,
  Have a bliss to die with, dim-descried.
This foot once planted on the goal,
This glory-garland round my soul,
Could I descry such? Try and test!
I sink back shuddering from the quest.
Earth being so good, would heaven seem best?
  Now, heaven and she are beyond this ride.

And yet—she has not spoke so long!
What if heaven be that, fair and strong
At life's best, with our eyes upturned
Whither life's flower is first discerned,
  We, fixed so, ever should so abide?
What if we still ride on, we two
With life for ever old yet new,
Changed not in kind but in degree,
The instant made eternity—
And heaven just prove that I and she
  Ride, ride together, for ever ride?

1899

Never the Time and the Place

NEVER the time and the place
 And the loved one all together!
This path—how soft to pace!
 This May—what magic weather!
Where is the loved one's face?
In a dream that loved one's face meets mine,
 But the house is narrow, the place is bleak
Where, outside, rain and wind combine
 With a furtive ear, if I strive to speak,
 With a hostile eye at my flushing cheek,
With a malice that marks each word, each sign!
O enemy sly and serpentine,
 Uncoil thee from the waking man!
  Do I hold the Past
  Thus firm and fast
 Yet doubt if the Future hold I can?
 This path so soft to pace shall lead
 Through the magic of May to herself indeed!
 Or narrow if needs the house must be,
 Outside are the storms and strangers: we—
Oh, close, safe, warm, sleep I and she, I and she.

1900

ROBERT BROWNING

Home-thoughts, from Abroad

OH, to be in England
   Now that April's there,
And whoever wakes in England
Sees, some morning, unaware,
That the lowest boughs and the brushwood sheaf
Round the elm-tree bole are in tiny leaf,
While the chaffinch sings on the orchard bough
In England—now!

And after April, when May follows,
And the whitethroat builds, and all the swallows!
Hark, where my blossomed pear-tree in the hedge
Leans to the field and scatters on the clover
Blossoms and dewdrops—at the bent spray's edge—
That's the wise thrush; he sings each song twice over,
Lest you should think he never could recapture
The first fine careless rapture!
And though the fields look rough with hoary dew,
All will be gay when noontide wakes anew
The buttercups, the little children's dower
—Far brighter than this gaudy melon-flower!

1901

ROBERT BROWNING

Andrea del Sarto

Called "The Faultless Painter"

*On the bare historical facts, as recorded by Vasari in the
life of the Florentine painter Andrea del Sarto, Browning
has framed this wonderful art-poem. Given those facts,
however, he has mixed them with his thought, and has
so transfigured the bare bones of biography that the sad,
infinitely pathetic soul, in its stunted growth and wasted
form, lives before us in the poem. As "Abt Vogler" is
his greatest music-poem, so this is Browning's greatest
painting-poem, and both are unique. If, says Berdoe,
Browning had written nothing but these two poems, "they
would suffice to insure immortality for their author." It
is said that the poem on Andrea was suggested by a picture in the Pitti Palace at Florence.*
*"Faultless but soulless", is the critical pronouncement
made upon Andrea's canvases. In this poem we are told
that Andrea's comparative failure as an artist was due
to his being an immoral man, infatuated with and de-
manding love of a woman who had neither heart nor intellect—a vampire. To provide money for her, he robbed
his patron, neglected his parents in their needy old age
and was otherwise derelict. Hence his failure, as the
poem makes plain.*

BUT do not let us quarrel any more,
   No, my Lucrezia; bear with me for once:
Sit down and all shall happen as you wish.
You turn your face, but does it bring your heart?
I'll work then for your friend's friend, never fear,
Treat his own subject after his own way,
Fix his own time, accept too his own price,

And shut the money into this small hand
When next it takes mine. Will it? tenderly?
Oh, I'll content him—but to-morrow, Love!
I often am much wearier than you think,
This evening more than usual, and it seems
As if—forgive now—should you let me sit
Here by the window with your hand in mine
And look a half-hour forth on Fiesole,
Both of one mind, as married people use,
Quietly, quietly the evening through,
I might get up to-morrow to my work
Cheerful and fresh as ever. Let us try.
To-morrow, how you shall be glad for this!
Your soft hand is a woman of itself,
And mine the man's bared breast she curls inside.
Don't count the time lost, neither; you must serve
For each of the five pictures we require:
It saves a model. So! keep looking so—
My serpentining beauty, rounds on rounds!
How could you ever prick those perfect ears,
Even to put the pearl there! oh, so sweet—
My face, my moon, my everybody's moon,
Which everybody looks on and calls his,
And, I suppose, is looked on by in turn,
While she looks—no one's: very dear, no less.
You smile? why, there's my picture ready made,
There's what we painters call our harmony!
A common grayness silvers everything—
All in a twilight, you and I alike—
You, at the point of your first pride in me
(That's gone, you know) but I, at every point;
My youth, my hope, my art, being all toned down
To yonder sober pleasant Fiesole.
There's the bell clinking from the chapel-top;
That length of convent-wall across the way

Holds the trees safer, huddled more inside;
The last monk leaves the garden; days decrease,
And Autumn grows, autumn in everything,
Eh? the whole seems to fall into a shape
As if I saw alike my work and self
And all that I was born to be and do,
A twilight-piece. Love, we are in God's hand.
How strange now looks the life he makes us lead;
So free we seem, so fettered fast we are!
I feel he laid the fetter: let it lie!
This chamber for example—turn your head—
All that's behind us! You don't understand
Nor care to understand about my art,
But you can hear at least when people speak;
And that cartoon, the second from the door:
It is the thing, Love! so such things should be—
Behold Madonna!—I am bold to say.
I can do with my pencil what I know,
What I see, what at bottom of my heart
I wish for, if I ever wish so deep—
Do easily, too—when I say, perfectly,
I do not boast, perhaps: yourself are judge.
Who listened to the Legate's talk last week,
And just as much they used to say in France.
At any rate 'tis easy, all of it!
No sketches first, no studies, that's long past:
I do what many dream of all their lives,
Dream? strive to do, and agonize to do,
And fail in doing. I could count twenty such
On twice your fingers, and not leave this town,
Who strive—you don't know how the others strive
To paint a little thing like that you smeared
Carelessly passing with your robes afloat—
Yet do much less, so much less, someone says,
(I know his name, no matter) so much less!

1904

Well, less is more, Lucrezia: I am judged.
There burns a truer light of God in them,
In their vexed beating stuffed and stopped-up brain,
Heart, or whate'er else, than goes on to prompt
This low-pulsed forthright craftsman's hand of mine.
Their works drop groundward, but themselves, I know,
Reach many a time a heaven that's shut to me,
Enter and take their place there sure enough,
Though they come back and cannot tell the world.
My works are nearer heaven, but I sit here.
The sudden blood of these men! at a word—
Praise them, it boils, or blame them, it boils too.
I, painting from myself and to myself,
Know what I do, am unmoved by men's blame
Or their praise either. Somebody remarks
Morello's outline there is wrongly traced,
His hue mistaken; what of that? or else,
Rightly traced and well ordered; what of that?
Speak as they please, what does the mountain care?
Ah, but a man's reach should exceed his grasp,
Or what's a heaven for? All is silver-gray
Placid and perfect with my art: the worse!
I know both what I want and what might gain,
And yet now profitless to know, to sigh
"Had I been two, another and myself,
Our head would have o'erlooked the world!" No doubt.
Yonder's a work now, of that famous youth
The Urbinate who died five years ago.
('Tis copied, George Vasari sent it me.)
Well, I can fancy how he did it all,
Pouring his soul, with kings and popes to see,
Reaching, that heaven might so replenish him,
Above and through his art—for it gives way;
That arm is wrongly put—and there again—
A fault to pardon in the drawing's lines,

1905

Its body, so to speak: its soul is right,
He means right—that, a child may understand.
Still, what an arm! and I could alter it:
But all the play, the insight and the stretch—
Out of me, out of me! And wherefore out?
Had you enjoined them on me, given me soul,
We might have risen to Rafael, I and you!
Nay, Love, you did give all I asked, I think—
More than I merit, yes, by many times.
But had you—oh, with the same perfect brow,
And perfect eyes, and more than perfect mouth,
And the low voice my soul hears, as a bird
The fowler's pipe, and follows to the snare—
Had you, with these the same, but brought a mind!
Some women do so. Had the mouth there urged
"God and the glory! never care for gain,
The present by the future, what is that?
Live for fame, side by side with Agnolo!
Rafael is waiting: up to God, all three!"
I might have done it for you. So it seems:
Perhaps not. All is as God overrules.
Beside, incentives come from the soul's self;
The rest avail not. Why do I need you?
What wife had Rafael, or has Agnolo?
In this world, who can do a thing, will not;
And who would do it, cannot, I perceive:
Yet the will's somewhat—somewhat, too, the power—
And thus we half-men struggle. At the end,
God, I conclude, compensates, punishes.
'Tis safer for me, if the award be strict,
That I am something underrated here,
Poor this long while, despised, to speak the truth.
I dared not, do you know, leave home all day,
For fear of chancing on the Paris lords.
The best is when they pass and look aside;

But they speak sometimes; I must bear it all.
Well may they speak! That Francis, that first time,
And that long festal year at Fontainebleau!
I surely then could sometimes leave the ground,
Put on the glory, Rafael's daily wear,
In that humane great monarch's golden look—
One finger in his beard or twisted curl
Over his mouth's good mark that made the smile,
One arm about my shoulder, round my neck,
The jingle of his gold chain in my ear,
I painting proudly with his breath on me,
All his court round him, seeing with his eyes,
Such frank French eyes, and such a fire of souls
Profuse, my hand kept plying by those hearts,
And, best of all, this, this, this face beyond,
This in the background, waiting on my work,
To crown the issue with a last reward!
A good time, was it not, my kingly days?
And had you not grown restless . . . but I know—
'Tis done and past; 'twas right, my instinct said;
Too live the life grew, golden and not gray,
And I'm the weak-eyed bat no sun should tempt
Out of the grange whose four walls make his world.
How could it end in any other way?
You called me, and I came home to your heart.
The triumph was—to reach and stay there; since
I reached it ere the triumph, what is lost?
Let my hands frame your face in your hair's gold,
You beautiful Lucrezia that are mine!
"Rafael did this, Andrea painted that;
The Roman's is the better when you pray,
But still the other's Virgin was his wife"—
Men will excuse me. I am glad to judge
Both pictures in your presence; clearer grows
My better fortune, I resolve to think.

1907

For, do you know, Lucrezia, as God lives,
Said one day Agnolo, his very self,
To Rafael . . . I have known it all these years . . .
(When the young man was flaming out his thoughts
Upon a palace-wall for Rome to see,
Too lifted up in heart because of it)
"Friend, there's a certain sorry little scrub
Goes up and down our Florence, none cares how,
Who, were he set to plan and execute
As you are, pricked on by your popes and kings,
Would bring the sweat into that brow of yours!"
To Rafael's!—And indeed the arm is wrong.
I hardly dare . . . yet, only you to see,
Give the chalk here—quick, thus the line should go!
Ay, but the soul! he's Rafael! rub it out!
Still, all I care for, if he spoke the truth,
(What he? why, who but Michel Agnolo?
Do you forget already words like those?)
If really there was such a chance so lost—
Is, whether you're—not grateful—but more pleased.
Well, let me think so. And you smile indeed!
This hour has been an hour! Another smile?
If you would sit thus by me every night
I should work better, do you comprehend?
I mean that I should earn more, give you more.
See, it is settled dusk now; there's a star;
Morello's gone, the watch-lights show the wall,
The cue-owls speak the name we call them by.
Come from the window, love—come in, at last,
Inside the melancholy little house
We built to be so gay with. God is just.
King Francis may forgive me: oft at nights
When I look up from painting, eyes tired out,
The walls become illumined, brick from brick

1908

Distinct, instead of mortar, fierce bright gold,
That gold of his I did cement them with!
Let us but love each other. Must you go?
That Cousin here again? he waits outside?
Must see you—you, and not with me? Those loans?
More gaming debts to pay? you smiled for that?
Well, let smiles buy me! have you more to spend?
While hand and eye and something of a heart
Are left me, work's my ware, and what's it worth?
I'll pay my fancy. Only let me sit
The grey remainder of the evening out,
Idle, you call it, and muse perfectly
How I could paint, were I but back in France,
One picture, just one more—the Virgin's face,
Not yours this time! I want you at my side
To hear them—that is, Michel Agnolo—
Judge all I do and tell you of its worth.
Will you? To-morrow, satisfy your friend.
I take the subjects for his corridor,
Finish the portrait out of hand—there, there,
And throw him in another thing or two
If he demurs; the whole should prove enough
To pay for this same Cousin's freak. Beside,
What's better and what's all I care about,
Get you the thirteen scudi for the ruff!
Love, does that please you? Ah, but what does he,
The Cousin! what does he to please you more?
I am grown peaceful as old age to-night.
I regret little, I would change still less.
Since there my past life lies, why alter it?
The very wrong to Francis!—it is true
I took his coin, was tempted and complied,
And built this house and sinned, and all is said.
My father and my mother died of want.

Well, had I riches of my own? you see
How one gets rich! Let each one bear his lot.
They were born poor, lived poor, and poor they died:
And I have laboured somewhat in my time
And not been paid profusely. Some good son
Paint my two hundred pictures—let him try!
No doubt, there's something strikes a balance. Yes,
You loved me quite enough, it seems to-night.
This must suffice me here. What would one have?
In heaven, perhaps, new chances, one more chance—
Four great walls in the New Jerusalem,
Meted on each side by the angel's reed,
For Leonard, Rafael, Agnolo and me
To cover—the three first without a wife,
While I have mine! So—still they overcome
Because there's still Lucrezia—as I choose.

Again the Cousin's whistle! Go, my Love.

1910

It's Wiser Being Good than Bad

IT'S wiser being good than bad;
  It's safer being meek than fierce;
It's fitter being sane than mad.
  My own hope is, a sun will pierce
The thickest cloud earth ever stretched
  That, after Last, returns the First,
Though a wide compass round be fetched;
  That what began best, can't end worst,
Nor what God blessed once, prove accurst.

The Boy and the Angel

*The story of the poor Italian boy who, morning, evening,
noon and night, ever sang "Praise God!" is most effectively told in this poem. It has no foreign foundation,
although it fully represents the Middle-Age spirit. Its lesson corresponds to the main idea in "Pippa Passes", that
"all service ranks the same with God", and therefore we
are not to seek to escape from any worthy task that may be
assigned us.*

MORNING, evening, noon and night,
  "Praise God!" sang Theocrite.

Then to his poor trade he turned,
Whereby the daily meal was earned.

Hard he labored, long and well;
O'er his work the boy's curls fell.

But ever, at each period,
He stopped and sang, "Praise God!"

1911

Then back again his curls he threw,
And cheerful turned to work anew.

Said Blaise, the listening monk, "Well done;
I doubt not thou art heard, my son,

"As well as if thy voice to-day
Here praising God, the Pope's great way.

"This Easter Day, the Pope at Rome
Praises God from Peter's dome."

Said Theocrite, "Would God that I
Might praise him that great way, and die!"

Night passed, day shone,
And Theocrite was gone.

With God a day endures alway,
A thousand years are but a day.

God said in heaven, "Nor day nor night
Now brings the voice of my delight."

Then Gabriel, like a rainbow's birth,
Spread his wings and sank to earth;

Entered, in flesh, the empty cell,
Lived there, and played the craftsman well;

And morning, evening, noon and night,
Praised God in place of Theocrite,

And from a boy, to youth he grew:
The man put off the stripling's hue;

1912

The man matured and fell away
Into the season of decay:

And ever over the trade he bent,
And ever lived on earth content.

(He did God's will; to him, all one
If on the earth or in the sun.)

God said, "A praise is in mine ear;
There is no doubt in it, no fear:

"So sing old worlds, and so
New worlds that from my footstool go.

"Clearer loves sound other ways:
I miss my little human praise."

Then forth sprang Gabriel's wings, off fell
The flesh disguise, remained the cell.

'Twas Easter Day: he flew to Rome,
And paused above Saint Peter's dome.

In the tiring-room close by
The great outer gallery,

With his holy vestments dight,
Stood the new Pope, Theocrite;

And all his past career
Came back upon him clear,

Since when, a boy, he plied his trade,
Till on his life the sickness weighed;

1913

And in his cell, when death drew near,
An angel in a dream brought cheer;

And rising from the sickness drear,
He grew a priest, and now stood here.

To the East with praise he turned,
And on his sight the angel burned.

"I bore thee from thy craftsman's cell,
And set thee here; I did not well.

"Vainly I left my angel-sphere,
Vain was thy dream of many a year.

"Thy voice's praise seemed weak; it dropped—
Creation's chorus stopped!

"Go back and praise again
The early way, while I remain.

"With that weak voice of our disdain,
Take up creation's pausing strain.

"Back to the cell and poor employ:
Resume the craftsman and the boy!"

Theocrite grew old at home;
A new Pope dwelt in Peter's dome.

One vanished as the other died:
They sought God side by side.

1914

Marching Along

FROM "CAVALIER TUNES"

KENTISH Sir Byng stood for his King,
  Bidding the crop-headed Parliament swing:
And, pressing a troop unable to stoop
And see the rogues flourish and honest folk droop,
Marched them along, fifty-score strong,
Great-hearted gentlemen, singing this song.

God for King Charles! Pym and such carles
To the Devil that prompts 'em their treasonous parles!
Cavaliers, up! Lips from the cup,
Hands from the pasty, nor bite take nor sup
Till you're—
    CHORUS.—Marching along, fifty-score strong,
              Great-hearted gentlemen, singing this
              song.

Hampden to hell, and his obsequies' knell.
Serve Hazelrig, Fiennes, and young Harry as well!
England, good cheer! Rupert is near!
Kentish and loyalists, keep we not here,
    CHORUS.—Marching along, fifty-score strong,
              Great-hearted gentlemen, singing this
              song?

Then, God for King Charles! Pym and his snarls
To the Devil that pricks on such pestilent carles!
Hold by the right, you double your might;
So, onward to Nottingham, fresh for the fight,
    CHORUS.—March we along, fifty-score strong,
              Great-hearted gentlemen, singing this
              song!

1915

ROBERT BROWNING

The Lost Leader

In his later years, Wordsworth seemed to lose his early revolutionary fervor; so Browning admitted that he had Wordsworth in mind in writing this poem, although it was not intended to be an exact portrait. Later in life Browning wrote: "I DID in my hasty youth presume to use the great and venerated personality of Wordsworth as a sort of painter's model; one from which this or the other particular feature may be selected and turned to account; had I intended more, above all, such a boldness as portraying the entire man, I should not have talked about 'handfuls of silver and bits of ribbon.' These never influenced the change of politics in the great poet, whose defection, nevertheless, accompanied as it was by a regular face-about of his special party, was to my juvenile apprehension, and even mature consideration, an event to deplore."

JUST for a handful of silver he left us,
    Just for a riband to stick in his coat—
Found the one gift of which fortune bereft us,
    Lost all the others she lets us devote;
They, with the gold to give, doled him out silver,
    So much was theirs who so little allowed;
How all our copper had gone for his service!
    Rags—were they purple, his heart had been proud!
We that had loved him so, followed him, honored him,
    Lived in his mild and magnificent eye,
Learned his great language, caught his clear accents,
    Made him our pattern to live and to die!
Shakespeare was of us, Milton was for us,
    Burns, Shelley, were with us—they watch from their
        graves!
He alone breaks from the van and the freemen—
    He alone sinks to the rear and the slaves!

1916

We shall march prospering—not through his presence;
  Songs may inspirit us—not from his lyre;
Deeds will be done—while he boasts his quiescence,
  Still bidding crouch whom the rest bade aspire.
Blot out his name, then, record one lost soul more,
  One task more declined, one more foot-path untrod,
One more devils'-triumph and sorrow for angels,
  One wrong more to man, one more insult to God!
Life's night begins: let him never come back to us!
  There would be doubt, hesitation and pain,
Forced praise on our part—the glimmer of twilight,
  Never glad confident morning again!
Best fight on well, for we taught him—strike gallantly,
  Menace our heart ere we master his own;
Then let him receive the new knowledge and wait us,
  Pardoned in heaven, the first by the throne!

A Woman's Last Word

LET'S contend no more, Love,
    Strive nor weep:
All be as before, Love,
    —Only sleep!

What so wild as words are?
    I and thou
In debate, as birds are,
    Hawk on bough!

1917

See the creatures stalking
   While we speak!
Hush and hide the talking,
   Cheek on cheek!

What so false as truth is,
   False to thee?
Where the serpent's tooth is,
   Shun the tree—

Where the apple reddens
   Never pry—
Lest we lose our Edens,
   Eve and I!

Be a god and hold me
   With a charm!
Be a man and fold me
   With thine arm!

Teach me, only teach, Love!
   As I ought
I will speak thy speech, Love,
   Think thy thought—

Meet, if thou require it,
   Both demands,
Laying flesh and spirit
   In thy hands.

That shall be to-morrow
   Not to-night:
I must bury sorrow
   Out of sight:

1918

Must a little weep, Love.
   (Foolish me!)
And so fall asleep, Love,
   Loved by thee.

How They Brought the Good News from Ghent to Aix

Browning says in a letter to an American inquirer that "there is no sort of historical foundation for the poem about 'Good News from Ghent.' I wrote it under the bulwark of a vessel, off the African coast, after I had been at sea long enough to appreciate even the fancy of a gallop on the back of a certain good horse 'York', then in my stable at home." Nevertheless, there was probably in his mind an event in the history of the Netherlands known as the Pacification of Ghent, which took place in 1576. There was a union of Holland, Zealand and the southern Netherlands, under William of Orange, to prosecute the struggle against Philip II of Spain.

I SPRANG to the stirrup, and Joris and he;
   I galloped, Dirck galloped, we galloped all three;
"Good speed!" cried the watch as the gatebolts undrew,
"Speed!" echoed the wall to us galloping through.
Behind shut the postern, the lights sank to rest,
And into the midnight we galloped abreast.

Not a word to each other; we kept the great pace—
Neck by neck, stride by stride, never changing our place;
I turned in my saddle and made its girths tight,
Then shortened each stirrup and set the pique right,
Rebuckled the check-strap, chained slacker the bit,
Nor galloped less steadily Roland a whit.

'Twas a moonset at starting; but while we drew near
Lokeren, the cocks crew and twilight dawned clear;
At Boom a great yellow star came out to see;
At Düffeld 'twas morning as plain as could be;
And from Mecheln church-steeple we heard the half-
    chime—
So Joris broke silence with "Yet there is time!"

At Aerschot up leaped of a sudden the sun,
And against him the cattle stood black every one,
To stare through the mist at us galloping past;
And I saw my stout galloper Roland at last.
With resolute shoulders, each butting away
The haze, as some bluff river headland its spray,

And his low head and crest, just one sharp ear bent
    back
For my voice, and the other pricked out on his track;
And one eye's black intelligence—ever that glance
O'er its white edge at me, his own master, askance;
And the thick heavy spume-flakes, which aye and anon
His fierce lips shook upward in galloping on.

By Hasselt, Dirck groaned; and cried Joris, "Stay spur!
Your Roos galloped bravely, the fault's not in her:
We'll remember at Aix"—for one heard the quick
    wheeze
Of her chest, saw the stretched neck, and staggering
    knees,
And sunk tail, and horrible heave of the flank,
As down on her haunches she shuddered and sank.

So we were left galloping, Joris and I,
Past Looz and past Tongres, no cloud in the sky;
The broad sun above laughed a pitiless laugh;

1920

'Neath our feet broke the brittle, bright stubble like
    chaff;
Till over by Dalhem a dome-spire sprang white,
And "Gallop," gasped Joris, "for Aix is in sight!"

"How they'll greet us!"—and all is in a moment his
    roan
Rolled neck and croup over, lay dead as a stone;
And there was my Roland to bear the whole weight
Of the news which alone could save Aix from her fate,
With his nostrils like pits full of blood to the brim,
And with circles of red for his eye-sockets' rim.

Then I cast loose my buff-coat, each holster let fall,
Shook off both my jack-boots, let go belt and all,
Stood up in the stirrup, leaned, patted his ear,
Called my Roland his pet name, my horse without peer—
Clapped my hands, laughed and sung, any noise, bad or
    good,
Till at length into Aix Roland galloped and stood.

And all I remember is, friends flocking round,
As I sate with his head 'twixt my knees on the ground;
And no voice but was praising this Roland of mine,
As I poured down his throat our last measure of wine,
Which (the burgesses voted by common consent)
Was no more than his due who brought good news
    from Ghent.

ROBERT BROWNING

Prologue to "The Two Poets of Croisic"

SUCH a starved bank of moss
   Till, that May-morn,
Blue ran the flash across:
   Violets were born!

Sky—what a scowl of cloud
   Till, near and far,
Ray on ray split the shroud:
   Splendid, a star!

World—how it walled about
   Life with disgrace
Till God's own smile came out:
   That was thy face!

1922

Evelyn Hope

BEAUTIFUL Evelyn Hope is dead!
  Sit and watch by her side an hour.
That is her book-shelf, this her bed;
  She plucked that piece of geranium-flower,
Beginning to die, too, in the glass.
  Little has yet been changed, I think:
The shutters are shut—no light may pass,
  Save two long rays through the hinge's chink.

Sixteen years old when she died!
  Perhaps she had scarcely heard my name:
It was not her time to love; beside,
  Her life had many a hope and aim,
Duties enough and little cares;
  And now was quiet, now astir—
Till God's hand beckoned unawares,
  And the sweet white brow is all of her.

Is it too late, then, Evelyn Hope?
  What! your soul was pure and true;
The good stars met in your horoscope,
  Made you of spirit, fire and dew;
And just because I was thrice as old,
  And our paths in the world diverged so wide,
Each was naught to each, must I be told?
  We were fellow-mortals—naught beside?

No, indeed! for God above
  Is great to grant, as mighty to make,
And creates the love to reward the love:
  I claim you still, for my own love's sake!

1923

Delayed, it may be, for more lives yet,
  Through worlds I shall traverse, not a few:
Much is to learn, and much to forget,
  Ere the time be come for taking you.

But the time will come—at last it will—
  When, Evelyn Hope, what meant, I shall say,
In the lower earth—in the years long still—
  That body and soul so pure and gay;
Why your hair was amber I shall divine,
  And your mouth of your own geranium's red—
And what you would do with me, in fine,
  In the new life come in the old one's stead.

I have lived, I shall say, so much since then,
  Given up myself so many times,
Gained me the gains of various men,
  Ransacked the ages, spoiled the climes;
Yet one thing—one—in my soul's full scope,
  Either I missed or itself missed me—
And I want and find you, Evelyn Hope!
  What is the issue? let us see!

I loved you, Evelyn, all the while;
  My heart seemed full as it could hold—
There was place and to spare for the frank young smile,
  And the red young mouth, and the hair's young gold,
So, hush! I will give you this leaf to keep:
  See, I shut it inside the sweet, cold hand.
There, that is our secret! go to sleep:
  You will wake, and remember, and understand.

1924

ROBERT BROWNING

By the Fireside

A middle-aged scholar is addressing his wife. "With whom else," he asks, "dare I look backward or dare pursue the path grey heads abhor?" The speaker has no dread of old age, because he has a soul-mate from whom not even death can separate him, and with the memory of this moment of irrevocable union he can face the bounds of life undaunted. The

> *"great brow*
> *And the spirit small hand propping it,"*

refer to Mrs. Browning; and the whole poem, though the incidents are imaginary, is thought to be a confession of his love for her and its influence on his own spiritual development. In this poem are touches of his fine philosophy, mounting to that memorable and immortal couplet:

> *"A little more, and how much it is—*
> *A little less, and what worlds away!"*

Are not the satisfactions of our lives ever dependent upon the "little more"; and our disappointments upon the "little less"? On some pages, how befogging our poet is; but on other pages, how quickening with light!

1925

ROBERT BROWNING

I

HOW well I know what I mean to do
  When the long dark autumn evenings come;
And where, my soul, is thy pleasant hue?
  With the music of all thy voices, dumb
In life's November too!

II

I shall be found by the fire, suppose,
  Over a great wise book, as beseemeth age;
While the shutters flap as the cross-wind blows,
  And I turn the page, and I turn the page,
Not verse now, only prose!

III

Till the young ones whisper, finger on lip,
  "There he is at it, deep in Greek:
Now then, or never, out we slip
  To cut from the hazels by the creek
A mainmast for our ship!"

IV

I shall be at it indeed, my friends!
  Greek puts already on either side
Such a branch-work forth as soon extends
  To a vista opening far and wide,
And I pass out where it ends.

1926

V

The outside frame, like your hazel-trees—
  But the inside-archway widens fast,
And a rarer sort succeeds to these,
  And we slope to Italy at last
And youth, by green degrees.

VI

I follow wherever I am led,
  Knowing so well the leader's hand:
O woman-country, wooed not wed,
  Loved all the more by earth's male-lands,
Laid to their hearts instead!

VII

Look at the ruined chapel again
  Half-way up in the Alpine gorge!
Is that a tower, I point you plain,
  Or is it a mill, or an iron forge
Breaks solitude in vain?

VIII

A turn, and we stand in the heart of things;
  The woods are round us, heaped and dim;
From slab to slab how it slips and springs,
  The thread of water single and slim,
Through the ravage some torrent brings!

1927

IX

Does it feed the little lake below?
　　The speck of white just on its marge
Is Pella; see, in the evening-glow,
　　How sharp the silver spear-heads charge
When Alp meets heaven in snow!

X

On our other side is the straight-up rock;
　　And a path is kept 'twixt the gorge and it
By boulder-stones where lichens mock
　　The marks on a moth, and small ferns fit
Their teeth to the polished block.

XI

Oh the sense of the yellow mountain-flowers,
　　And thorny balls, each three in one,
The chestnuts throw on our path in showers!
　　For the drop of the woodland fruit's begun,
These early November hours,

XII

That crimson the creeper's leaf across
　　Like a splash of blood, intense, abrupt,
O'er a shield else gold from rim to boss,
　　And lay it for show on the fairy-cupped
Elf-needled mat of moss,

1928

XIII

By the rose-flesh mushrooms, undivulged
   Last evening—nay, in to-day's first dew
Yon sudden coral nipple bulged,
   Where a freaked fawn-colored flaky crew
Of toad-stools peep indulged.

XIV

And yonder, at foot of the fronting ridge
   That takes the turn to a range beyond,
Is the chapel reached by the one-arched bridge,
   Where the water is stopped in a stagnant pond
Danced over by the midge.

XV

The chapel and bridge are of stone alike,
   Blackish-grey and mostly wet;
Cut hemp-stalks steep in the narrow dyke.
   See here again, how the lichens fret
And the roots of the ivy strike!

XVI

Poor little place, where its one priest comes
   On a festa-day, if he comes at all,
To the dozen folk from their scattered homes,
   Gathered within that precinct small
By the dozen ways one roams—

1929

XVII

To drop from the charcoal-burners' huts,
  Or climb from the hemp-dresser's low shed,
Leave the grange where the woodman stores his nuts,
  Or the wattled cote where the fowlers spread
Their gear on the rock's bare juts.

XVIII

It has some pretension too, this front,
  With its bit of fresco half-moon-wise
Set over the porch, Art's early wont:
  'Tis John in the Desert, I surmise,
But has borne the weather's brunt—

XIX

Not from the fault of the builder, though,
  For a pent-house properly projects
Where three carved beams make a certain show,
  Dating—good thought of our architect's—
Five, six, nine, he lets you know.

XX

And all day long a bird sings there,
  And a stray sheep drinks at the pond at times;
The place is silent and aware;
  It has had its scenes, its joys and crimes,
But that is its own affair.

1930

XXXVII

Oh, moment one and infinite!
  The water slips o'er stock and stone;
The West is tender, hardly bright:
  How grey at once is the evening grown—
One star, its chrysolite!

XXXVIII

We two stood there with never a third,
  But each by each, as each knew well:
The sights we saw and the sounds we heard,
  The lights and the shades made up a spell
Till the trouble grew and stirred.

XXXIX

Oh, the little more, and how much it is!
  And the little less, and what worlds away!
How a sound shall quicken content to bliss,
  Or a breath suspend the blood's best play,
And life be a proof of this!

XL

Had she willed it, still had stood the screen
  So slight, so sure, 'twixt my love and her:
I could fix her face with a guard between,
  And find her soul as when friends confer,
Friends—lovers that might have been.

1935

XLI

For my heart had a touch of the woodland time,
    Wanting to sleep now over its best.
Shake the whole tree in the summer-prime,
    But bring to the last leaf no such test!
"Hold the last fast!" runs the rhyme.

XLII

For a chance to make your little much,
    To gain a lover and lose a friend,
Venture the tree and a myriad such,
    When nothing you mar but the year can mend:
But a last leaf—fear to touch!

XLIII

Yet should it unfasten itself and fall
    Eddying down till it find your face
At some slight wind—best chance of all!
    Be your heart henceforth its dwelling-place
You trembled to forestall!

XLIV

Worth how well, those dark grey eyes,
    That hair so dark and dear, how worth
That a man should strive and agonize,
    And taste a veriest hell on earth
For the hope of such a prize!

1936

ROBERT BROWNING

XLV

You might have turned and tried a man,
  Set him a space to weary and wear,
And prove which suited more your plan,
  His best of hope or his worst despair,
Yet end as he began.

XLVI

But you spared me this, like the heart you are,
  And filled my empty heart at a word.
If two lives join, there is oft a scar,
  They are one and one, with a shadowy third;
One near one is too far.

XLVII

A moment after, and hands unseen
  Were hanging the night around us fast;
But we knew that a bar was broken between
  Life and life: we were mixed at last
In spite of the mortal screen.

XLVIII

The forests had done it; there they stood;
  We caught for a moment the powers at play:
They had mingled us so, for once and good,
  Their work was done—we might go or stay,
They relapsed to their ancient mood.

1937

XLIX

How the world is made for each of us!
   How all we perceive and know in it
Tends to some moment's product thus,
   When a soul declares itself—to wit,
By its fruit, the thing it does!

L

Be hate that fruit or love that fruit,
   It forwards the general deed of man:
And each of the Many helps to recruit
   The life of the race by a general plan;
Each living his own, to boot.

LI

I am named and known by that moment's feat;
   There took my station and degree;
So grew my own small life complete,
   As nature obtained her best of me—
One born to love you, sweet!

LII

And to watch you sink by the fireside **now**
   Back again, as you mutely sit
Musing by firelight, that great brow
   And the spirit-small hand propping **it**,
Yonder, my heart knows how!

1938

LIII

So, earth has gained by one man the more,
    And the gain of earth must be heaven's gain too;
And the whole is well worth thinking o'er
    When autumn comes: which I mean to do
One day, as I said before.

Count Gismond

*This poem is based upon a Provençal legend, and is
wholly imaginary, but it gives an admirable picture of
the times of chivalry. Arthur Symons says: "The medi-
aeval temper of entire confidence in the ordeal by duel has
never been better rendered."*

AIX IN PROVENCE

I

CHRIST God who savest man, save most
    Of men Count Gismond who saved me!
Count Gauthier, when he choose his post,
    Chose time and place and company
To suit it; when he struck at length
My honor, 'twas with all his strength.

II

And doubtlessly, ere he could draw
    All points to one, he must have schemed!
That miserable morning saw
    Few half so happy as I seemed,
While being dressed in queen's array
To give our tourney prize away.

1939

III

I thought they loved me, did me grace
  To please themselves; 'twas all their deed
God makes, or fair or foul, our face:
  If showing mine so caused to bleed
My cousins' hearts, they should have dropped
A word, and straight the play had stopped.

IV

They, too, so beauteous! Each a queen
  By virtue of her brow and breast;
Not needing to be crowned, I mean,
  As I do. Even when I was dressed,
Had either of them spoke, instead
Of glancing sideways with still head!

V

But no: they let me laugh, and sing
  My birthday song quite through, adjust
The last rose in my garland, fling
  A last look on the mirror, trust
My arms to each an arm of theirs,
And so descend the castle-stairs—

VI

And come out on the morning troop
  Of merry friends who kissed my cheek,
And called me queen, and made me stoop
  Under the canopy—(a streak
That pierced it, of the outside sun,
Powdered with gold its gloom's soft dun)

1940

VII

And they could let me take my state
  And foolish throne amid applause
Of all come there to celebrate
  My queen's-day—Oh, I think the cause
Of much was, they forgot no crowd
Makes up for parents in their shroud!

VIII

However that be, all eyes were bent
  Upon me, when my cousins cast
Theirs down, 'twas time I should present
  The victor's crown, but . . . there, 'twill last
No long time . . . the old mist again
Blinds me as then it did. How vain!

IX

See! Gismond's at the gate, in talk
  With his two boys: I can proceed.
Well, at that moment, who should stalk
  Forth boldly—to my face, indeed—
But Gauthier? and he thundered "Stay!"
And all stayed. "Bring no crowns, I say!

X

"Bring torches! Wind the penance-sheet
  "About her! Let her shun the chaste,
"Or lay herself before their feet!
  "Shall she, whose body I embraced
"A night long, queen it in the day?
"For honor's sake no crowns, I say!"

1941

XI

I? What I answered? As I live,
  I never fancied such a thing
As answer possible to give.
  What says the body when they spring
Some monstrous torture-engine's whole
Strength on it? No more says the soul.

XII

Till out strode Gismond; then I knew
  That I was saved. I never met
His face before, but, at first view,
  I felt quite sure that God had set
Himself to Satan: who would spend
A minute's mistrust on the end?

XIII

He strode to Gauthier, in his throat
  Gave him the lie, then struck his mouth
With one back-handed blow that wrote
  In blood men's verdict there. North, South,
East, West, I looked. The lie was dead,
And damned, and truth stood up instead.

XIV

This glads me most, that I enjoyed
  The heart o' the joy, with my content
In watching Gismond unalloyed
  By any doubt of the event:
God took that on him—I was bid
Watch Gismond for my part: I did.

1942

XV

Did I not watch him while he let
  His armorer just brace his greaves,
Rivet his hauberk, on the fret
  The while! His foot . . . my memory leaves
No least stamp out, nor how anon
He pulled his ringing gauntlets on.

XVI

And e'en before the trumpet's sound
  Was finished, prone lay the false knight
Prone as his lie, upon the ground:
  Gismond flew at him, used no sleight
O' the sword, but open-breasted drove,
Cleaving till out the truth he clove.

XVII

Which done, he dragged him to my feet
  And said, "Here die, but end thy breath
"In full confession, lest thou fleet
  "From my first, to God's second death!
"Say, hast thou lied?" And, "I have lied
"To God and her," he said, and died.

XVIII

Then Gismond, kneeling to me, asked
  What safe my heart holds, though no word
Could I repeat now, if I tasked
  My powers for ever, to a third
Dear even as you are. Pass the rest
Until I sank upon his breast.

1943

XIX

Over my head his arm he flung
　　Against the world; and scarce I felt
His sword (that dripped by me and swung)
　　A little shifted in its belt:
For he began to say the while
How South our home lay many a mile.

XX

So, 'mid the shouting multitude
　　We two walked forth to never more
Return.　My cousins have pursued
　　Their life, untroubled as before
I vexed them.　Gauthier's dwelling-place,
God lighten!　May his soul find grace!

XXI

Our elder boy has got the clear
　　Great brow; though when his brother's black
Full eye shows scorn, it . . . Gismond here?
　　And have you brought my tercel back?
I was just telling Adela
How many birds it struck since May.

1944

ROBERT BROWNING

A Grammarian's Funeral

SHORTLY AFTER THE REVIVAL OF LEARNING IN EUROPE

Here we have a faithful description of the love of learning manifested by the scholarly pioneers of the Renaissance. The word "grammarian" then had a larger meaning than it has come to have, for it signified a student in the wider sense, one devoted to letters or general learning. As R. H. Hutton says, in his "Literary Essays": "The aim of this poem is to bring out the strong, implicit faith in an eternal career, which there must be in any man who devotes his life wholly to the preliminary toil of mastering the rudiments of language."

LET us begin and carry up this corpse,
    Singing together.
Leave we the common crofts, the vulgar thorps
    Each in its tether
Sleeping safe on the bosom of the plain,
    Cared-for till cock-crow:
Look out if yonder be not day again
    Rimming the rock-row!
That's the appropriate country; there, man's thought,
    Rarer, intenser,
Self-gathered for an outbreak, as it ought,
    Chafes in the censer.
Leave we the unlettered plain its herd and crop;
    Seek we sepulture
On a tall mountain, citied to the top,
    Crowded with culture!
All the peaks soar, but one the rest excels;
    Clouds overcome it;
No! yonder sparkle is the citadel's
    Circling its summit.

Thither our path lies; wind we up the heights;
    Wait ye the warning?
Our low life was the level's and the night's;
    He's for the morning.
Step to a tune, square chests, erect each head,
    'Ware the beholders!
This is our master, famous, calm and dead,
    Borne on our shoulders.

Sleep, crop and herd! sleep, darkling thorp and croft,
    Safe from the weather!
He, whom we convoy to his grave aloft,
    Singing together,
He was a man born with thy face and throat,
    Lyric Apollo!
Long he lived nameless: how should Spring take note
    Winter would follow?
Till lo, the little touch, and youth was gone!
    Cramped and diminished,
Moaned he, "New measures, other feet anon!
    My dance is finished?"
No, that's the world's way: (keep the mountain-side,
    Make for the city!)
He knew the signal, and stepped on with pride
    Over men's pity;
Left play for work, and grappled with the world
    Bent on escaping:
"What's in the scroll," quoth he, "thou keepest furled?
    Show me their shaping,
Theirs who most studied man, the bard and sage—
    Give!"—So, he gowned him,
Straight got by heart that book to its last page:
    Learnèd, we found him.
Yea, but we found him bald too, eyes like lead,
    Accents uncertain:

"Time to taste life," another would have said,
    "Up with the curtain!"
This man said rather, "Actual life comes next?
    Patience a moment!
Grant I have mastered learning's crabbèd text,
    Still there's the comment.
Let me know all! Prate not of most or least,
    Painful or easy!
Even to the crumbs I'd fain eat up the feast,
    Ay, nor feel queasy."
Oh, such a life as he resolved to live,
    When he had learned it,
When he had gathered all books had to give!
    Sooner, he spurned it.
Imagine the whole, then execute the parts—
    Fancy the fabric
Quite, ere you build, ere steel strike fire from quartz,
    Ere mortar dab brick!
(Here's the town-gate reached: there's the market-place
    Gaping before us.)
Yea, this in him was the peculiar grace
    (Hearten our chorus!)
That before living he'd learn how to live—
    No end to learning:
Earn the means first—God surely will contrive
    Use for our earning.
Others mistrust and say, "But time escapes:
    Live now or never!"
He said, "What's time? Leave Now for dogs and apes!
    Man has Forever."
Back to his book then: deeper drooped his head:
    Calculus racked him:
Leaden before, his eyes grew dross of lead:
    Tussis attacked him.

1947

"Now, master, take a little rest!"—not he!
 (Caution redoubled,
Step two abreast, the way winds narrowly!)
 Not a whit troubled,
Back to his studies, fresher than at first,
 Fierce as a dragon
He (soul-hydroptic with a sacred thirst)
 Sucked at the flagon.
Oh, if we draw a circle premature,
 Heedless of far gain,
Greedy for quick returns of profit, sure
 Bad is our bargain!
Was it not great? did not he throw on God
 (He loves the burthen)
God's task to make the heavenly period
 Perfect the earthen?
Did not he magnify the mind, show clear
 Just what it all meant?
He would not discount life, as fools do here,
 Paid by instalment.
He ventured neck or nothing—heaven's success
 Found, or earth's failure:
"Wilt thou trust death or not?" He answered "Yes!
 Hence with life's pale lure!"
That low man seeks a little thing to do,
 Sees it and does it:
This high man, with a great thing to pursue,
 Dies ere he knows it.
This low man goes on adding one to one,
 His hundred's soon hit:
This high man, aiming at a million,
 Misses an unit.
That, has the world here—should he need the next,
 Let the world mind him!

1948

This, throws himself on God, and unperplexed
    Seeking shall find him.
So, with the throttling hands of death at strife,
    Ground he at grammar;
Still, through the rattle, parts of speech were rife:
    While he could stammer
He settled *Hoti's* business—let it be!—
    Properly based *Oun*—
Gave us the doctrine of the enclitic *De,*
    Dead from the waist down.
Well, here's the platform, here's the proper place:
    Hail to your purlieus,
All ye highfliers of the feathered race,
    Swallows and curlews!
Here's the top-peak; the multitude below
    Live, for they can, there:
This man decided not to Live but Know—
    Bury this man there?
Here—here's his place, where meteors shoot, clouds
      form,
    Lightnings are loosened,
Stars come and go! Let joy break with the storm,
    Peace let the dew send!
Lofty designs must close in like effects:
    Loftily lying,
Leave him—still loftier than the world suspects,
    Living and dying.

ROBERT BROWNING

Memorabilia
(1792–1822)

AH, did you once see Shelley plain,
  And did he stop and speak to you,
And did you speak to him again?
  How strange it seems and new!

But you were living before that,
  And also you were living after;
And the memory I started at—
  My starting moves your laughter!

I crossed a moor, with a name of its own
  And a certain use in the world no doubt;
Yet a hand's-breath of it shines alone
  'Mid the blank miles round about.

For there I picked up on the heather
  And there I put inside my breast
A molted feather, an eagle-feather!
  Well, I forget the rest.

In a Year

NEVER any more
  While I live,
Need I hope to see his face
  As before.
Once his love grown chill,
  Mine may strive—
Bitterly we re-embrace,
  Single still.

1950

Was it something said,
        Something done,
Vexed him? was it touch of hand,
        Turn of head?
Strange! that very way
        Love begun.
I as little understand
        Love's decay.

When I sewed or drew,
        I recall
How he looked as if I sang—
        Sweetly too.
If I spoke a word,
        First of all
Up his cheek the color sprang,
        Then he heard.

Sitting by my side,
        At my feet,
So he breathed the air I breathed,
        Satisfied!
I, too, at love's brim
        Touched the sweet:
I would die if death bequeathed
        Sweet to him.

"Speak—I love thee best!"
        He exclaimed.
"Let thy love my own foretell—"
        I confessed:
"Clasp my heart on thine
        Now unblamed,
Since upon thy soul as well
        Hangeth mine!"

Was it wrong to own,
  Being truth?
Why should all the giving prove
  His alone?
I had wealth and ease,
  Beauty, youth—
Since my lover gave me love,
  I gave these.

That was all I meant—
  To be just,
And the passion I had raised
  To content.
Since he chose to change
  Gold for dust,
If I gave him what he praised,
  Was it strange?

Would he loved me yet,
  On and on,
While I found some way undreamed,
  Paid my debt!
Gave more life and more,
  Till, all gone,
He should smile, "She never seemed
  Mine before.

"What—she felt the while,
  Must I think?
Love's so different with us men,"
  He should smile.
"Dying for my sake—
  White and pink!
Can't we touch these bubbles then
  But they break?"

1952

Dear, the pang is brief.
    Do thy part,
Have thy pleasure. How perplext
    Grows belief!
Well, this cold clay clod
    Was man's heart.
Crumble it—and what comes next?
    Is it God?

After

TAKE the cloak from his face, and at first
    Let the corpse do its worst.

How he lies in his rights of a man!
    Death has done all death can.
And, absorbed in the new life he leads,
    He recks not, he heeds
Nor his wrong nor my vengeance—both strike
    On his senses alike,
And are lost in the solemn and strange
    Surprise of the change.

Ha, what avails death to erase
    His offense, my disgrace?
I would we were boys as of old
    In the field, by the fold:
His outrage, God's patience, man's scorn
    Were so easily borne.

I stand here now, he lies in his place:
    Cover the face.

1953

ROBERT BROWNING

The Pied Piper of Hamelin

Browning wrote these verses as a diversion for the young son of William Macready, the actor-manager, who produced one or two plays by the great poet-dramatist. Its author seems to have thought the poem of little value. It was taken more or less literally from "The Wonders of the Little World", by Nathanial Wanley, published in 1678. Several other accounts may have, or have not, been known to Browning, but in any event the story of the Pied Piper is nothing more than a myth of the wind. The poem is a masterpiece of its narrative kind.

I

HAMELIN town's in Brunswick,
　　By famous Hanover city;
　The river Weser, deep and wide,
　Washes its wall on the southern side;
　　A pleasanter spot you never spied,
But when begins my ditty,
　　Almost five hundred years ago,
　　To see the townsfolk suffer so
From vermin, was a pity.

II

　　Rats!
They fought the dogs, and killed the cats,
　And bit the babies in the cradles,
And ate the cheeses out of the vats,
　And licked the soup from the cook's own ladles,
Split open the kegs of salted sprats,
Made nests inside men's Sunday hats,

And even spoiled the women's chats,
　　By drowning their speaking
　　With shrieking and squeaking
In fifty different sharps and flats.

III

At last the people in a body
　　To the Town Hall came flocking:
" 'Tis clear," cried they, "our Mayor's noddy;
　　And as for our Corporation—shocking
To think we buy gowns lined with ermine
For dolts that can't or won't determine,
What's best to rid us of our vermin!
You hope, because you're old and obese,
To find in the furry civic robe ease.
Rouse up, Sirs! Give your brains a racking
To find the remedy we're lacking,
Or, sure as fate, we'll send you packing!"
At this the Mayor and Corporation
Quaked with a mighty consternation.

IV

An hour they sate in counsel—
　　At length the Mayor broke silence:
"For a guilder I'd my ermine gown sell;
　　I wish I were a mile hence!
It's easy to bid one rack one's brain—
I'm sure my poor head aches again,
I've scratched it so, and all in vain.
Oh for a trap, a trap, a trap!"
Just as he said this, what should hap
At the chamber door but a gentle tap?
"Bless us," cried the Mayor, "what's that?"

(With the Corporation as he sat,
Looking little, though wondrous fat;
Nor brighter was his eye, nor moister
Than a too-long-opened oyster,
Save when at noon his paunch grew mutinous
For a plate of turtle, green and glutinous)
"Only a scraping of shoes on the mat?
Anything like the sound of a rat
Makes my heart go pit-a-pat!"

V

"Come in!"—the Mayor cried, looking bigger:
And in did come the strangest figure!
His queer long coat from heel to head
Was half of yellow and half of red;
And he himself was tall and thin;
With sharp blue eyes, each like a pin;
And light loose hair, yet swarthy skin;
No tuft on cheek nor beard on chin,
But lips where smiles went out and in—
There was no guessing his kith and kin!
And nobody could enough admire
The tall man and his quaint attire.
Quoth one: "It's as my great-grandsire,
Starting up at the Trump of Doom's tone,
Had walked this way from his painted tombstone!"

VI

He advanced to the council-table:
And, "Please your honors," said he, "I'm able,
By means of a secret charm, to draw
All creatures living beneath the sun,

That creep, or swim, or fly, or run,
After me so as you never saw!
And I chiefly use my charm
On creatures that do people harm—
The mole, and toad, and newt, and viper—
And people call me the Pied Piper."
(And here they noticed round his neck
A scarf of red and yellow stripe,
To match with his coat of the self-same check;
And at the scarf's end hung a pipe;
And his fingers, they noticed, were ever straying
As if impatient to be playing
Upon this pipe, as low it dangled
Over his vesture so old-fangled.)
"Yet," said he, "poor piper as I am,
In Tartary I freed the Cham,
Last June, from his huge swarm of gnats;
I eased in Asia the Nizam
Of a monstrous brood of vampire-bats;
And, as for what your brain bewilders—
If I can rid your town of rats,
Will you give me a thousand guilders?"
"One? fifty thousand!"—was the exclamation
Of the astonished Mayor and Corporation.

VII

Into the street the Piper stept,
    Smiling first a little smile,
As if he knew what magic slept
    In his quiet pipe the while;
Then, like a musical adept,
To blow the pipe his lips he wrinkled,
And green and blue his sharp eyes twinkled,
Like a candle flame where salt is sprinkled.

And ere three shrill notes the pipe uttered,
You heard as if an army muttered;
And the muttering grew to a grumbling;
And the grumbling grew to mighty rumbling;
And out of the houses the rats came tumbling.
Great rats, small rats, lean rats, brawny rats,
Brown rats, black rats, grey rats, tawny rats,
Grave old plodders, gay young friskers,
    Fathers, mothers, uncles, cousins,
Cocking tails and pricking whiskers;
    Families by tens and dozens,
Brothers, sisters, husbands, wives—
Followed the Piper for their lives.
From street to street he piped advancing,
And step for step they followed dancing,
Until they came to the river Weser,
Wherein all plunged and perished—
Save one who, stout as Julius Cæsar,
Swam across and lived to carry
(As he the manuscript he cherished)
To Rat-land home his commentary,
Which was: "At the first shrill notes of the pipe,
I heard a sound as of scraping tripe,
And putting apples, wondrous ripe,
Into a cider-press's gripe—
And a moving away of pickle-tub-boards,
And a leaving ajar of conserve-cupboards,
And a drawing the corks of train-oil-flasks,
And a breaking the hoops of butter-casks;
And it seemed as if a voice
(Sweeter far than by harp or by psaltery
Is breathed) called out, O rats, rejoice!
The world is grown to one vast drysaltery!
So munch on, crunch on, take your nuncheon,
Breakfast, supper, dinner, luncheon!

1958

And just as a bulky sugar-puncheon,
All ready staved, like a great sun shone
Glorious, scarce an inch before me,
Just as methought it said, come, bore me!—
I found the Weser rolling o'er me."

VIII

You should have heard the Hamelin people
Ringing the bells till they rocked the steeple;
"Go," cried the Mayor, "and get long poles!
Poke out the nests and block up the holes!
Consult with carpenters and builders,
And leave in our town not even a trace
Of the rats!"—when suddenly up the face
Of the Piper perked in the market-place,
With a "First, if you please, my thousand guilders!"

IX

A thousand guilders! The Mayor looked blue;
So did the Corporation too.
For council dinners made rare havoc
With Claret, Moselle, Vin-de-Grave, Hock;
And half the money would replenish
Their cellar's biggest butt with Rhenish.
To pay this sum to a wandering fellow
With a gipsy coat of red and yellow!
"Beside," quoth the Mayor, with a knowing wink,
"Our business was done at the river's brink;
We saw with our eyes the vermin sink,
And what's dead can't come to life, I think.
So, friend, we're not the folks to shrink
From the duty of giving you something for drink,

And a matter of money to put in your poke;
But, as for the guilders, what we spoke
Of them, as you very well know, was in joke.
Beside, our losses have made us thrifty;
A thousand guilders! Come, take fifty!"

X

The piper's face fell, and he cried,
"No trifling! I can't wait! beside,
I've promised to visit by dinner time
Bagdat, and accept the prime
Of the Head Cook's pottage, all he's rich in,
For having left, in the Caliph's kitchen,
Of a nest of scorpions no survivor—
With him I proved no bargain-driver;
With you, don't think I'll bate a stiver!
And folks who put me in a passion
May find me pipe to another fashion."

XI

"How?" cried the Mayor, "d'ye think I'll brook
Being worse treated than a cook?
Insulted by a lazy ribald
With idle pipe and vesture piebald?
You threaten us, fellow? Do your worst,
Blow your pipe there till you burst!"

XII

Once more he stept into the street;
    And to his lips again
    Laid his long pipe of smooth straight cane;
And ere he blew three notes (such sweet

Soft notes as yet musician's cunning
  Never gave the enraptured air)
There was a rustling that seemed like a bustling
Of merry crowds justling at pitching and hustling;
Small feet were pattering, wooden shoes clattering,
Little hands clapping, and little tongues chattering;
And, like fowls in a farm-yard when barley is scat-
    tering,
Out came the children running.
All the little boys and girls,
With rosy cheeks and flaxen curls,
And sparkling eyes and teeth like pearls,
Tripping and skipping, ran merrily after
The wonderful music with shouting and laughter.

XIII

The Mayor was dumb, and the Council stood
As if they were changed into blocks of wood,
Unable to move a step, or cry
To the children merrily skipping by—
And could only follow with the eye
That joyous crowd at the Piper's back.
But how the Mayor was on the rack,
And the wretched Council's bosoms beat,
As the Piper turned from the High Street
To where the Weser rolled its waters
Right in the way of their sons and daughters!
However, he turned from South to West,
And to Koppelberg Hill his steps addressed,
And after him the children pressed;
Great was the joy in every breast.
"He never ran cross that mighty top!
He's forced to let the piping drop,
And we shall see our children stop!"

When, lo, as they reached the mountain's side,
A wondrous portal opened wide,
As if a cavern was suddenly hollowed;
And the Piper advanced and the children followed;
And when all were in, to the very last,
The door in the mountain side shut fast.
Did I say all? No! One was lame,
And could not dance the whole of the way!
And in after years, if you would blame
His sadness, he was used to say:
"It's dull in our town since my playmates left!
I can't forget that I'm bereft
Of all the pleasant sights they see,
Which the Piper also promised me;
For he led us, he said, to a joyous land,
Joining the town and just at hand,
Where waters gushed and fruit-trees grew,
And flowers put forth a fairer hue,
And everything was strange and new;
The sparrows were brighter than peacocks here,
And their dogs outran our fallow deer,
And honey-bees had lost their stings,
And horses were born with eagles' wings.
And just as I became assured
My lame foot would be speedily cured,
The music stopped and I stood still,
And found myself outside the Hill,
Left alone against my will,
To go now limping as before,
And never hear of that country more!"

XIV

Alas, alas for Hamelin!
    There came into many a burgher's pate

A text which says, that Heaven's gate
Opes to the rich at as easy a rate
As the needle's eye takes a camel in!
The Mayor sent East, West, North, and South,
To offer the piper by word of mouth,
    Wherever it was men's lot to find him,
Silver and gold to his heart's content,
If he'd only return the way he went,
    And bring the children behind him.
But when they saw 'twas a lost endeavor,
And Piper and dancers were gone forever,
They made a decree that lawyers never
    Should think their records dated duly
If, after the day of the month and year,
These words did not as well appear,
    "And so long after what happened here
    On the Twenty-second of July,
Thirteen Hundred and Seventy-six:"
And the better in memory to fix
The place of the children's last retreat
They called it the Pied Piper's Street—
Where any one playing on pipe or tabor
Was sure for the future to lose his labor.
Nor suffered they hostelry or tavern
    To shock with mirth a street so solemn;
But opposite the place of the cavern
    They wrote the story on a column,
And on the Great Church window painted
The same, to make the world acquainted
How their children were stolen away;
And there it stands to this very day.

And I must not omit to say
That in Transylvania there's a tribe
Of alien people, that ascribe

The outlandish ways and dress
On which their neighbors lay such stress
To their fathers and mothers having risen
Out of some subterranean prison,
Into which they were trepanned
Long time ago, in a mighty band,
Out of Hamelin town in Brunswick land,
But how or why, they don't understand.

xv

So, Willy, let you and me be wipers
Of scores out with all men—especially pipers;
And, whether they pipe us free from rats or from
      mice,
If we promised them aught, let us keep our promise.

From "Rabbi Ben Ezra"

*Ibn Ezra, upon whose life and philosophy this poem is
based, was one of the most eminent of the Jewish scholars
of the Middle Ages. He was born in Spain. Much of
his philosophy, as attested by his writings, has been absorbed and effectively rendered by Browning in this poem.
For instance, when the Rabbi of the poem speaks of the
body at its best projecting the soul on its way, he is voic-
ing Ibn Ezra, who says: "It is well known that, as long
as the bodily desires are strong, the soul is weak and
powerless against them, because they are supported by the
body and all its powers: hence those who think only of
eating and drinking will never be wise. . . . The soul is
not yet prepared for pure knowledge, on account of the
animal which seeks dominion and enkindles passion; therefore after the victory gained with the support of the
animal over the desires, it is necessary that the soul should*

ROBERT BROWNING

devote itself to wisdom, and seek its support for the sub-jection of the passions, in order to remain under the sole control of knowledge."

GROW old along with me!
  The best is yet to be,
The last of life, for which the first was made:
Our times are in his hand
Who saith, "A whole I planned,
Youth shows but half; trust God: see all, nor be
      afraid!"

Rejoice we are allied
To that which doth provide
And not partake, effect and not receive!
A spark disturbs our clod;
Nearer we hold of God
Who gives, than of his tribes that take, I must believe.

Then, welcome each rebuff
That turns earth's smoothness rough,
Each sting that bids nor sit nor stand but go!
Be our joys three-parts pain!
Strive, and hold cheap the strain;
Learn, nor account the pang; dare, never grudge the
      throe!

Let us not always say,
"Spite of this flesh to-day
I strove, made head, gained ground upon the whole!"
As the bird wings and sings,
Let us cry, "All good things
Are ours, nor soul helps flesh more, now, than flesh
      helps soul!"

1965

Youth ended, I shall try
My gain or loss thereby:
Leave the fire ashes, what survives is gold;
And I shall weigh the same,
Give life its praise or blame:
Young, all lay in dispute: I shall know, being old.

Enough now, if the Right
And Good and Infinite
Be named here, as thou callest thy hand thine own,
With knowledge absolute,
Subject to no dispute
From fools that crowded youth, nor let thee feel alone.

Now, who shall arbitrate?
Ten men love what I hate,
Shun what I follow, slight what I receive;
Ten, who in ears and eyes
Match me; we all surmise,
They this thing, and I that: whom shall my soul
    believe?

Not on the vulgar mass
Called "work," must sentence pass,
Things done, that took the eye and had the price;
O'er which, from level stand,
The low world laid its hand,
Found straightway to its mind, could value in a trice:

But all, the world's coarse thumb
And finger failed to plumb,
So passed in making up the main account:

1966

All instincts immature
All purposes unsure,
That weighed not as his work, yet swelled the man's
    amount:

Thoughts hardly to be packed
Into a narrow act,
Fancies that broke through language and escaped:
All I could never be,
All, men ignored in me,
This, I was worth to God, whose wheel the pitcher
    shaped.

Look not thou down but up!
To uses of a cup,
The festal board, lamp's flash and trumpet's peal,
The new wine's foaming flow,
The Master's lips aglow!
Thou, heaven's consummate cup, what needst thou with
    earth's wheel?

But I need, now as then,
Thee, God, who moldest men;
And since, not even while the whirl was worst,
Did I—to the wheel of life
With shapes and colors rife,
Bound dizzily—mistake my end, to slake thy thirst:

So, take and use thy work:
Amend what flaws may lurk,
What strain o' the stuff, what warpings past the aim.
My times be in thy hand,
Perfect the cup as planned!
Let age approve of youth, and death complete the same!

ROBERT BROWNING

Incident of the French Camp

The incident upon which this touching poem is based took place at the storming of Ratisbon, in Bavaria, by Napoleon in 1809.

I

YOU know, we French stormed Ratisbon:
   A mile or so away,
On a little mound, Napoleon
   Stood on our storming-day:
With neck out-thrust, you fancy how,
   Legs wide, arms locked behind,
As if to balance the prone brow
   Oppressive with its mind.

II

Just as perhaps he mused "My plans
   That soar, to earth may fall,
Let once my army-leader Lannes
   Waver at yonder wall"—
Out 'twixt the battery-smokes there flew
   A rider, bound on bound
Full-galloping; nor bridle drew
   Until he reached the mound.

III

Then off there flung in smiling joy,
  And held himself erect
By just his horse's mane, a boy:
  You hardly could suspect—
(So tight he kept his lips compressed,
  Scarce any blood came through)
You looked twice ere you saw his breast
  Was all but shot in two.

IV

"Well," cried he, "Emperor, by God's grace
  We've got you Ratisbon!
The Marshal's in the market-place,
  And you'll be there anon
To see your flag-bird flap his vans
  Where I, to heart's desire,
Perched him!" The chief's eye flashed; his plans
  Soared up again like fire.

V

The chief's eye flashed; but presently
  Softened itself, as sheathes
A film the mother-eagle's eye
  When her bruised eaglet breathes.
"You're wounded!" "Nay," the soldier's pride
  Touched to the quick, he said:
"I'm killed, Sire!" And his chief beside,
  Smiling the boy fell dead.

ROBERT BROWNING

"Childe Roland to the Dark Tower Came"

Here, in "Childe Roland", we reach a poem that stands at the summit of Browning's genius. It is "of imagination all compact"; and in the range of its vision and in the energy of its dramatic drive, coupled with its weird beauty, it surpasses all poems since "Christabel" and "The Ancient Mariner." It is all laid in the hard clay and granite of realism; and yet it is molded with such magic as to seem to be an adventure in the world of the supernatural. Nothing in Dante surpasses the gray terror of its figures and the naked terror of its landscapes.

He begins his search on the main-traveled road, but the cripple directs him to press out into the pathless wilderness: he must leave the beaten roads of the world.

The poem seems to rise as by some sorcery out of a single simple line sung by Edgar, the pretended madman in "King Lear"—

> *"Childe Roland to the dark tower came."*

This bold adventurer is one of the few remaining of an eager band who have attempted to reach the mysterious tower. He resolves on one last endeavor, which involves many wanderings over stretches of gloom and evil omen— ever beset by unearthly loneliness and vague apprehension—beset by a sense of the terror and sorrows in mortal things. At last the hero reaches the goal,

> *"The round squat tower, blind as the fool's heart."*

Here he beholds the ghosts of the baffled seekers of the past, all watching for his destruction, even as they had been destroyed:

> *"In a sheet of flame,*
> *I saw them and I knew them all. And yet*
> *Dauntless the slug-horn to my lips I set."*

1970

ROBERT BROWNING

*And what does it all mean? To me, it signifies the diffi-
cult and desperate quest for the Ideal, found only on the
untrodden trails. Browning himself was asked whether
his central aim was to express constancy to an ideal—"he
that endureth to the end shall be saved"—and the poet
replied, "Yes, just about that." Indeed, even with the
universe against a man, he must sound his militant challenge, and press on to his goal.*

I

MY first thought was, he lied in every word,
 That hoary cripple, with malicious eye
Askance to watch the working of his lie
On mine, and mouth scarce able to afford
Suppression of the glee, that pursed and scored
 Its edge, at one more victim gained thereby.

II

What else should he be set for, with his staff?
 What save to waylay with his lies, ensnare
 All travelers who might find him posted there,
And ask the road? I guessed what skull-like laugh
Would break, what crutch 'gin write my epitaph
 For pastime in the dusty thoroughfare,

III

If at his counsel I should turn aside
 Into that ominous tract which, all agree,
 Hides the Dark Tower. Yet acquiescingly
I did turn as he pointed: neither pride
Nor hope rekindling at the end descried,
 So much as gladness that some end might be.

1971

IV

For, what with my whole world-wide wandering,
    What with my search drawn out through years, my
        hope
    Dwindled into a ghost not fit to cope
With that obstreperous joy success would bring—
I hardly tried now to rebuke the spring
    My heart made, finding failure in its scope.

V

As when a sick man very near to death
    Seems dead indeed, and feels begin and end
    The tears, and takes the farewell of each friend,
And hears one bid the other go, draw breath
Freelier outside ("Since all is o'er," he saith,
    "And the blow fallen no grieving can amend.")

VI

While some discuss if near the other graves
    Be room enough for this, and when a day
    Suits best for carrying the corpse away,
With care about the banners, scarves, and staves:
And still the man hears all, and only craves
    He may not shame such tender love and stay.

VII

Thus, I had so long suffered in this quest,
    Heard failure prophesied so oft, been writ
    So many times among "The Band"—to wit,
The knights who to the Dark Tower's search addressed

Their steps—that just to fail as they, seemed best,
   And all the doubt was now—should I be fit?

VIII

So, quiet as despair, I turned from him,
   That hateful cripple, out of his highway
   Into the path he pointed. All the day
Had been a dreary one at best, and dim
Was settling to its close, yet shot one grim
   Red leer to see the plain catch its estray.

IX

For mark! no sooner was I fairly found
   Pledged to the plain, after a pace or two,
   Than, pausing to throw backward a last view
Over the safe road, 'twas gone; gray plain all round:
Nothing but plain to the horizon's bound.
   I might go on; naught else remained to do.

X

So, on I went. I think I never saw
   Such starved ignoble nature; nothing throve:
   For flowers—as well expect a cedar grove!
But cockle, spurge, according to their law
Might propagate their kind, with none to awe,
   You'd think; a burr had been a treasure trove.

XI

No! penury, inertness, and grimace,
   In some strange sort, were the land's portion. "See
   Or shut your eyes," said Nature peevishly,

"It nothing skills: I cannot help my case:
'Tis the Last Judgment's fire must cure this place,
 Calcine its clods and set my prisoners free."

XII

If there pushed any ragged thistle-stalk
 Above its mates, the head was chopped; the bents
 Were jealous else. What made those holes and rents
In the dock's harsh swarth leaves, bruised as to balk
All hope of greenness? 'tis a brute must walk
 Pashing their life out, with a brute's intents.

XIII

As for the grass, it grew as scant as hair
 In leprosy; thin dry blades pricked the mud
 Which underneath looked kneaded up with blood.
One stiff blind horse, his every bone a-stare,
Stood stupefied, however he came there:
 Thrust out past service from the devil's stud.

XIV

Alive! he might be lead for aught I know,
 With that red gaunt and colloped neck a-strain,
 And shut eyes underneath the rusty mane;
Seldom went such grotesqueness with such woe;
I never saw a brute I hated so;
 He must be wicked to deserve such pain.

XV

I shut my eyes and turned them on my heart.
 As a man calls for wine before he fights,

I asked one draught of earlier, happier sights,
Ere fitly I could hope to play my part.
Think first, fight afterwards—the soldier's art:
  One taste of the old time sets all to rights.

XVI

Not it! I fancied Cuthbert's reddening face
  Beneath its garniture of curly gold,
  Dear fellow, till I almost felt him fold
An arm in mine to fix me to the place,
That way he used. Alas, one night's disgrace!
  Out went my heart's new fire and left it cold.

XVII

Giles then, the soul of honor—there he stands
  Frank as ten years ago when knighted first.
  What honest man should dare (he said) he durst.
Good—but the scene shifts—faugh! what hangman
    hands
Pin to his breast a parchment? His own bands
  Read it. Poor traitor, spit upon and curst!

XVIII

Better this present than a past like that;
  Back therefore to my darkening path again!
  No sound, no sight as far as eye could strain.
Will the night send a howlet or a bat?
I asked: when something on the dismal flat
  Came to arrest my thoughts and change their train.

1975

XIX

A sudden little river crossed my path
  As unexpected as a serpent comes.
  No sluggish tide congenial to the glooms;
This, as it frothed by, might have been a bath
For the fiend's glowing hoof—to see the wrath
  Of its black eddy bespate with flakes and spumes.

XX

So petty yet so spiteful! All along,
  Low scrubby alders kneeled down over it;
  Drenched willows flung them headlong in a fit
Of mute despair, a suicidal throng:
The river which had done them all the wrong,
  Whate'er that was, rolled by, deterred no whit.

XXI

Which, while I forded, good saints, how I feared,
  To set my foot upon a dead man's cheek,
  Each step, or feel the spear I thrust to seek
For hollows tangled in his hair or beard!
It may have been a water-rat I speared,
  But, ugh! it sounded like a baby's shriek.

XXII

Glad was I when I reached the other bank.
  Now for a better country. Vain presage!
  Who were the strugglers, what war did they wage
Whose savage trample thus could pad the dank
Soil to a plash? Toads in a poisoned tank,
  Or wild cats in a red-hot iron cage—

XXIII

The fight must so have seemed in that fell cirque.
  What penned them there, with all the plain to choose?
  No foot-print leading to that horrid mews,
None of it. Mad brewage set to work
Their brains, no doubt, like galley-slaves the Turk
  Pits for his pastime, Christians against Jews.

XXIV

And more than that—a furlong on—why, there!
  What bad use was that engine for, that wheel,
  Or brake, not wheel—that harrow fit to reel
Men's bodies out like silk? with all the air
Of Tophet's tool, on earth left unaware,
  Or brought to sharpen its rusty teeth of steel.

XXV

Then came a bit of stubbed ground, once a wood,
  Next a marsh, it would seem, and now mere earth
  Desperate and done with (so a fool finds mirth,
Makes a thing and then mars it, till his mood
Changes and off he goes!) within a rood—
  Bog, clay, and rubble, sand and stark black dearth.

XXVI

Now blotches rankling, colored gay and grim,
  Now patches where some leanness of the soil's
  Broke into moss or substances like boils;
Then came some palsied oak, a cleft in him
Like a distorted mouth that split its rim
  Gaping at death, and dies while it recoils.

1977

XXVII

And just as far as ever from the end!
  Naught in the distance but the evening, naught
   To point my footstep further! At the thought,
A great black bird, Apollyon's bosom-friend,
Sailed past, nor beat his wide wing dragon-penned
   That brushed my cap—perchance the guide I sought.

XXVIII

For, looking up, aware I somehow grew,
  'Spite of the dusk, the plain had given place
   All round to mountains—with such name to grace
Mere ugly heights and heaps now stolen in view.
How thus they had surprised me,—solve it, you!
   How to get from them was no clearer case.

XXIX

Yet half I seemed to recognize some trick
  Of mischief happened to me, God knows when—
   In a bad dream perhaps. Here ended, then,
Progress this way. When, in the very nick
Of giving up, one time more, came a click
   As when a trap shuts—you're inside the den.

XXX

Burningly it came on me all at once,
  This was the place! those two hills on the right,
   Crouched like two bulls locked horn in horn in fight,
While, to the left, a tall scalped mountain . . . Dunce,
Dotard, a-dozing at the very nonce,
   After a life spent training for the sight!

XXXI

What in the midst lay but the Tower itself?
  The round squat turret, blind as the fool's heart,
  Built of brown stone, without a counterpart
In the whole world. The tempest's mocking elf
Points to the shipman thus the unseen shelf
  He strikes on, only when the timbers start.

XXXII

Not see? because of night perhaps? Why, day
  Came back again for that! before it left,
  The dying sunset kindled through a cleft:
The hills, like giants at a hunting, lay,
Chin upon hand, to see the game at bay.
  "Now stab and end the creature—to the heft!"

XXXIII

Not hear? when noise was everywhere! it tolled
  Increasing like a bell. Names in my ears
  Of all the lost adventures my peers—
How such a one was strong, and such was bold,
And such was fortunate, yet each of old
  Lost, lost! one moment knelled the woe of years.

XXXIV

There they stood, ranged along the hill-sides, met
  To view the last of me, a living frame
  For one more picture! in a sheet of flame
·I saw them and I knew them all. And yet
Dauntless the slug-horn to my lips I set,
  And blew, *"Childe Roland to the Dark Tower came."*

1979

ROBERT BROWNING

Abt Vogler

(After He Has Been Extemporizing upon the Musical Instrument of His Invention)

George Joseph Vogler, a Catholic priest (hence Abt or Abbé) was an organist and composer, born at Würzburg, Bavaria, in 1749. Opinion differs regarding his merits as a musician, some music scholars holding him to have had originality and genius, others pronouncing him a charlatan. He was an eccentric and visionary, but played an important part in the development of musical science and in making music popular. His visionary character, his remarkable talent as an extemporizer and his religious calling are impressively celebrated in this wonderful poem.

I

WOULD that the structure brave, the manifold
    music I build,
  Bidding my organ obey, calling its keys to their work,
Claiming each slave of the sound, at a touch, as when
    Solomon willed
  Armies of angels that soar, legions of demons that
    lurk,
Man, brute, reptile, fly—alien of end and of aim,
  Adverse, each from the other heaven-high, hell-deep
    removed—
Should rush into sight at once as he named the in-
    effable Name,
  And pile him a palace straight, to pleasure the prin-
    cess he loved!

II

Would it might tarry like his, the beautiful building
    of mine,

This which my keys in a crowd pressed and im-
  portuned to raise!
Ah, one and all, how they helped, would dispart now
    and now combine,
  Zealous to hasten the work, heighten their master
    his praise!
And one would bury his brow with a blind plunge down
    to Hell,
  Burrow a while and build, broad on the roots of
    things,
Then up again swim into sight, having based me my
    palace well,
  Founded it, fearless of flame, flat on the nether
    springs.

III

And another would mount and march, like the excel-
    lent minion he was,
  Ay, another and yet another, one crowd but with
    many a crest,
Raising my rampired walls of gold as transparent as
    glass,
  Eager to do and die, yield each his place to the rest:
For higher still and higher (as a runner tips with fire,
  When a great illumination surprises a festal night—
Outlining round and round Rome's dome from space to
    spire)
  Up, the pinnacled glory reached, and the pride of
    my soul was in sight.

IV

In sight? Not half! for it seemed, it was certain, to
    match man's birth,

Nature in turn conceived, obeying an impulse as I;
And the emulous heaven yearned down, made effort to
    reach the earth,
  As the earth had done her best, in my passion, to
    scale the sky:
Novel splendors burst forth, grew familiar and dwelt
    with mine,
  Not a point nor peak but found and fixed its wan-
    dering star;
Meteor-moons, balls of blaze: and they did not pale
    nor pine,
  For earth had attained to heaven, there was no more
    near nor far.

v

Nay more; for there wanted not who walked in the
    glare and glow,
  Presences plain in the place; or, fresh from the Pro-
    toplast,[1]
Furnished for ages to come, when a kindlier wind
    should blow,
  Lured now to begin and live, in a house to their
    liking at last:
Or else the wonderful Dead who have passed through
    the body and gone,
  But were back once more to breathe in an old world
    worth their new:
What never had been, was now; what was, as it shall
    be anon;
  And what is—shall I say, matched both? for I was
    made perfect too.

[1] The thing first formed as a model to be copied.

VI

All through my keys that gave their sounds to a wish
of my soul,
  All through my soul, that praised as its wish flowed
visibly forth,
All through music and me! For think, had I painted
the whole,
  Why, there it had stood, to see, nor the process so
wonder-worth:
Had I written the same, made verse—still, effect pro-
ceeds from cause:
  Ye know why the forms are fair, ye hear how the
tale is told;
It is all triumphant art, but art in obedience to laws,
  Painter and poet are proud in the artist-list enrolled.

VII

But here is the finger of God, a flash of the will that
can,
  Existent behind all laws: that made them, and, lo,
they are!
And I know not if, save in this, such gift be allowed to
man,
  That out of three sounds he frame, not a fourth
sound, but a star.
Consider it well: each tone of our scale in itself is
naught;
  It is everywhere in the world—loud, soft, and all is
said:
Give it to me to use! I mix it with two in my thought:
  And, there! Ye have heard and seen: consider and
bow the head!

VIII

Well, it is gone at last, the palace of music I reared;
  Gone! and the good tears start, the praises that come
    too slow;
For one is assured at first, one scarce can say that he
    feared,
  That he even gave it a thought, the gone thing was
    to go.
Never to be again! But many more of the kind
  As good, nay, better perchance: is this your comfort
    to me?
To me, who must be saved, because I cling with my
    mind
  To the same, same self-same love, same God: ay,
    what was, shall be.

IX

Therefore to whom turn I but to thee, the ineffable
    Name?
  Builder and maker, Thou, of houses not made with
    hands!
What, have fear of change from Thee who art ever the
    same?
  Doubt that Thy power can fill the heart that Thy
    power expands?
There shall never be one lost good! What was, shall
    live as before;
  The evil is null, is naught, is silence implying sound;
What was good, shall be good, with, for evil, so much
    good more;
  On the earth the broken arcs; in the heaven, a per-
    fect round.

X

All we have willed or hoped or dreamed of good, shall
  exist;
  Not its semblance, but itself; no beauty, nor good,
  nor power
Whose voice has gone forth, but each survives for the
  melodist
  When eternity affirms the conception of an hour.
The high that proved too high, the heroic for earth too
  hard,
  The passion that left the ground to lose itself in the
  sky
Are music sent up to God by the lover and the bard;
  Enough that he heard it once: we shall hear it by-
  and-by.

XI

And what is our failure here but a triumph's evidence
  For the fulness of the days? Have we withered or
  agonized?
Why else was the pause prolonged but that singing
  might issue thence?
  Why rushed the discords in, but that harmony should
  be prized?
Sorrow is hard to bear, and doubt is slow to clear,
  Each sufferer says his say, his scheme of the weal
  and woe;
But God has a few of us whom he whispers in the ear;
  The rest may reason and welcome; 'tis we musicians
  know.

1985

XII

Well, it is earth with me; silence resumes her reign;
  I will be patient and proud, and soberly acquiesce.
Give me the keys. I feel for the common chord again,
  Sliding by semitones, till I sink to the minor—yes,
And I blunt it into a ninth, and I stand on alien ground,
  Surveying awhile the heights I rolled from into the
    deep;
Which, hark, I have dared and done, for my resting-
    place is found,
  The C Major [1] of this life: so, now I will try to sleep.

---

[1] Miss Helen Ormerod, in a paper read before the Browning Society of London, has explained these musical terms as follows: C Major is what may be called the natural scale, having no sharps or flats in its signature. Pauer says that minor keys are chosen for expressing intense seriousness, soft melancholy, longing, sadness and passionate grief; whilst major keys, with sharps and flats in their signatures, are said to have distinctive qualities—perhaps Browning chose C Major for the key, as the one most applied to matters of everyday life.

ROBERT BROWNING

My Last Duchess

FERRARA

THAT'S my last Duchess painted on the wall,
    Looking as if she were alive. I call
That piece a wonder, now: Frà Pandolf's hands
Worked busily a day, and there she stands.
Will 't please you sit and look at her? I said
"Frà Pandolf" by design, for never read
Strangers like you that pictured countenance,
The depth and passion of its earnest glance,
But to myself they turned (since none puts by
The curtain I have drawn for you, but I)
And seemed as they would ask me, if they durst
How such a glance came there; so, not the first
Are you to turn and ask thus. Sir, 't was not
Her husband's presence only, called that spot
Of joy into the Duchess' cheek: perhaps
Frà Pandolf chanced to say, "Her mantle laps
Over my lady's wrist too much," or "Paint
Must never hope to reproduce the faint
Half-flush that dies along her throat:" such stuff
Was courtesy, she thought, and cause enough
For calling up that spot of joy. She had
A heart—how shall I say?—too soon made glad.
Too easily impressed: she liked whate'er
She looked on, and her looks went everywhere.
Sir, 't was all one! My favor at her breast,
The dropping of the daylight in the West,
The bough of cherries some officious fool
Broke in the orchard for her, the white mule
She rode with round the terrace—all and each

Would draw from her alike the approving speech,
Or blush, at least.   She thanked men—good! but
    thanked
Somehow—I know not how—as if she ranked
My gift of a nine-hundred-years-old name
With anybody's gift.   Who'd stoop to blame
This sort of trifling?   Even had you skill
In speech—(which I have not)—to make your will
Quite clear to such an one, and say, "Just this
Or that in you disgusts me; here you miss,
Or there exceed the mark"—and if she let
Herself be lessoned so, nor plainly set
Her wits to yours, forsooth, and made excuse,
Even then would be some stooping; and I choose
Never to stoop.   Oh sir, she smiled, no doubt,
Whenever I passed her; but who passed without
Much the same smile?   This grew; I gave commands;
Then all smiles stopped together.   There she stands
As if alive.   Will 't please you rise?   We'll meet
The company below, then.   I repeat,
The Count your master's known munificence
Is ample warrant that no just pretence
Of mine for dowry will be disallowed;
Though his fair daughter's self, as I avowed
At starting, is my object.   Nay, we'll go
Together down, sir.   Notice Neptune, though,
Taming a sea-horse, thought a rarity,
Which Claus of Innsbruck cast in bronze for me!

ROBERT BROWNING

The Bishop Orders his Tomb at Saint Praxed's Church

ROME, 15—

Ruskin said of this poem: "I know no other piece of modern English, prose or poetry, in which there is so much told, as in these lines, of the Renaissance spirit—its worldliness, inconsistency, pride, hypocrisy, ignorance of itself, love of art, of luxury, and of good Latin. It is nearly all that I said of the central Renaissance in thirty pages of the 'Stones of Venice', put into as many lines, Browning's being also the antecedent work. The worst of it is that this kind of concentrated writing needs so much solution before the reader can fairly get the good of it, that people's patience fails them, and they give the thing up as insoluble; though, truly, it ought to be to the current of common thought like Saladin's talisman, dipped in clear water, not soluble altogether, but making the element medicinal."

VANITY, saith the preacher, vanity!
   Draw round my bed: is Anselm keeping back?
Nephews—sons mine . . . ah God, I know not! Well—
She, men would have to be your mother once,
Old Gandolf envied me, so fair she was!
What's done is done, and she is dead beside,
Dead long ago, and I am Bishop since,
And as she died so must we die ourselves,
And thence ye may perceive the world's a dream.
Life, how and what is it? As here I lie
In this state-chamber, dying by degrees,
Hours and long hours in the dead night, I ask
"Do I live, am I dead?" Peace, peace seems all.
Saint Praxed's ever was the church for peace;
And so, about this tomb of mine. I fought

With tooth and nails to save my niche, ye know:
Old Gandolf cozened me, despite my care;
Shrewd was that snatch from out the corner South
He graced his carrion with, God curse the same!
Yet still my niche is not so cramped but thence
One sees the pulpit o' the epistle-side,
And somewhat of the choir, those silent seats,
And up into the aery dome where live
The angels, and a sunbeam's sure to lurk;
And I shall fill my slab of basalt there,
And 'neath my tabernacle take my rest,
With those nine columns round me, two and two,
The odd one at my feet where Anselm stands:
Peach-blossom marble all, the rare, the ripe
As fresh-poured red wine of a mighty pulse.
Old Gandolf with his paltry onion-stone,
Put me where I may look at him! True peach,
Rosy and flawless: how I earned the prize!
Draw close: that conflagration of my church—
What then? So much was saved if aught were missed!
My sons, ye would not be my death? Go dig
The white-grape vineyard where the oil-press stood,
Drop water gently till the surface sink,
And if ye find . . . Ah God, I know not, I! . . .
Bedded in store of rotten fig-leaves soft,
And corded up in a tight olive-frail,
Some lump, ah God, of *lapis lazuli,*
Big as a Jew's head cut off at the nape,
Blue as a vein o'er the Madonna's breast.
Sons, all have I bequeathed you, villas, all,
That brave Frascati villa with its bath,
So, let the blue lump poise between my knees,
Like God the Father's globe on both his hands
Ye worship in the Jesu Church so gay,
For Gandolf shall not choose but see and burst!

1990

Swift as a weaver's shuttle fleet our years:
Man goeth to the grave, and where is he? . . .
Did I say basalt for my slab, sons? Black—
'Twas ever antique-black I meant! How else
Shall ye contrast my frieze to come beneath?
The bas-relief in bronze ye promised me.
Those Pans and Nymphs ye wot of, and perchance
Some tripod, thyrsus, with a vase or so,
The Saviour at his sermon on the mount,
Saint Praxed in a glory, and one Pan
Ready to twitch the Nymph's last garment off,
And Moses with the tables . . . but I know
Ye mark me not! What do they whisper thee,
Child of my bowels, Anselm? Ah, ye hope
To revel down my villas while I gasp
Bricked o'er with beggar's mouldy travertine
Which Gandolf from his tomb-top chuckles at!
Nay, boys, ye love me—all of jasper, then!
'Tis jasper ye stand pledged to, lest I grieve.
My bath must needs be left behind, alas!
One block, pure green as a pistachio-nut,
There's plenty jasper somewhere in the world—
And have I not Saint Praxed's ear to pray
Horses for ye, and brown Greek manuscripts,
And mistresses with great smooth marbly limbs?
That's if ye carve my epitaph aright,
Choice Latin, picked phrase, Tully's every word,
No gaudy ware like Gandolf's second line—
Tully, my masters? Ulpian serves his need!
And then how I shall lie through centuries,
And hear the blessed mutter of the mass,
And see God made and eaten all day long,
And feel the steady candle-flame, and taste
Good strong thick stupefying incense-smoke!
For as I lie here, hours of the dead night,

Dying in state and by such slow degrees,
I fold my arms as if they clasped a crook,
And stretch my feet forth straight as stone can point,
And let the bedclothes, for a mortcloth, drop
Into great laps and folds of sculptor's-work;
And as yon tapers dwindle, and strange thoughts
Grow, with a certain humming in my ears,
About the life before I lived this life,
And this life too, popes, cardinals and priests,
Saint Praxed at his sermon on the mount,
Your tall pale mother with her talking eyes,
And new-found agate urns as fresh as day,
And marble's language, Latin pure, discreet—
Aha, ELUCESCEBRAT quoth our friend?
No Tully, said I, Ulpian at the best!
Evil and brief hath been my pilgrimage.
All *lapis,* all, sons! Else I give the Pope
My villas! Will ye ever eat my heart? . . .
Ever your eyes were as a lizard's quick,
They glitter like your mother's for my soul,
Or ye would heighten my impoverished frieze,
Piece out its starved design, and fill my vase
With grapes, and add a visor and a Term,
And to the tripod ye would tie a lynx
That in his struggle throws the thyrsus down,
To comfort me on my entablature
Whereon I am to lie till I must ask
"Do I live, am I dead?" There, leave me, there!
For ye have stabbed me with ingratitude
To death—ye wish it—God, ye wish it! Stone—
Gritstone, a-crumble! Clammy squares which sweat
As if the corpse they keep were oozing through—
And no more *lapis* to delight the world!
Well, go! I bless ye. Fewer tapers there,
But in a row: and, going, turn your backs—

Ay, like departing altar-ministrants,
And leave me in my church, the church for peace,
That I may watch at leisure if he leers—
Old Gandolf—at me, from his onion-stone,
As still he envied me, so fair she was!

Two in the Campagna

I WONDER do you feel to-day
  As I have felt since, hand in hand,
We sat down on the grass, to stray
  In spirit better through the land,
This morn of Rome and May?

For me, I touched a thought, I know,
  Has tantalized me many times,
(Like turns of thread the spiders throw
  Mocking across our path) for rhymes
To catch at and let go.

Help me to hold it! First it left
  The yellowing fennel, run to seed
There, branching from the brickwork's cleft,
  Some old tomb's ruin; yonder weed
Took up the floating weft,

Where one small orange cup amassed
  Five beetles—blind and green they grope
Among the honey-meal; and last,
  Everywhere on the grassy slope
I traced it. Hold it fast!

The champaign with its endless fleece
    Of feathery grasses everywhere!
Silence and passion, joy and peace,
    An everlasting wash of air—
Rome's ghost since her decease.

Such life here, through such lengths of hours,
    Such miracles performed in play,
Such primal naked forms of flowers,
    Such letting nature have her way,
While heaven looks from its towers!

How say you? Let us, O my dove,
    Let us be unashamed of soul,
As earth lies bare to heaven above!
    How is it under our control
To love or not to love?

I would that you were all to me,
    You that are just so much, no more.
Nor yours nor mine, nor slave nor free!
    Where does the fault lie? What the core
O' the wound, since wound must be?

I would I could adopt your will,
    See with your eyes, and set my heart
Beating by yours, and drink my fill
    At your soul's springs—your part my part
In life, for good and ill.

No, I yearn upward, touch you close,
    Then stand away. I kiss your cheek,
Catch your soul's warmth—I pluck the rose
    And love it more than tongue can speak—
Then the good minute goes.

1994

Already how am I so far
　　Out of that minute?　Must I go
Still like the thistle-ball, no bar,
　　Onward, whenever light winds blow,
Fixed by no friendly star?

Just when I seemed about to learn!
　　Where is the thread now?　Off again!
The old trick!　Only I discern—
　　Infinite passion, and the pain
Of finite hearts that yearn.

Love in a Life

ROOM after room,
　I hunt the house through
We inhabit together.
Heart, fear nothing, for, heart, thou shalt find her—
Next time, herself!—not the trouble behind her
Left in the curtain, the couch's perfume!
As she brushed it, the cornice-wreath blossomed anew:
Yon looking-glass gleamed at the wave of her feather.

Yet the day wears,
And door succeeds door;
I try the fresh fortune—
Range the wide house from the wing to the center.
Still the same chance! she goes out as I enter.
Spend my whole day in the quest—who cares?
But 'tis twilight, you see—with such suites to explore,
Such closets to search, such alcoves to importune!

Life in a Love

E SCAPE me?
    Never—
Beloved!
While I am I, and you are you,
  So long as the world contains us both,
  Me the loving and you the loth,
While the one eludes must the other pursue.
My life is a fault at last, I fear:
  It seems too much like a fate, indeed!
  Though I do my best I shall scarce succeed.
But what if I fail of my purpose here?
It is but to keep the nerves at strain,
  To dry one's eyes and laugh at a fall,
And baffled, get up and begin again;
  So the chase takes up one's life, that's all.

The Statue and the Bust

*The Riccardi Palace in Florence is the scene of the story
told here of the love between Duke Ferdinand and the wife
of Riccardi, both eminent Florentines. The result is de-
scribed in the poem. The husband kept his young wife a
virtual prisoner when he apprehended the liaison. From
her palace-prison bedroom she could see and be seen of
her lover only when she gazed from the windows. In
revenge, Ferdinand erected his statue, that he might always
appear to watch for the fair one. This tradition Browning
expands and embellishes with great dramatic effect. The
fact that the relations of the lovers were platonic is estab-
lished. But, as Berdoe says: "The Duke would have
been more manly and the woman truer to her human instincts if he and she had let love have its way. Both*

*dwarfed and withered their souls by looking and longing
and pining for what they had not courage to grasp. The
sin in each case was as great in the sight of God." It
was simply prudence and conventionality which restrained
the lovers; and these things count for nothing with the
poet-psychologist. But conventionality counts for a great
deal in our conduct of life. It may have been "the crown-
ing disaster to miss life" for the man and woman: if so,
it was a sacrifice justly due to human society.*

THERE'S a palace in Florence, the world knows
    well,
And a statue watches it from the square.
And this story of both do our townsmen tell.

Ages ago, a lady there,
At the farthest window facing the East
Asked, "Who rides by with the royal air!"

The bridesmaids' prattle around her ceased;
She leaned forth, one on either hand;
They saw how the blush of the bride increased—

They felt by its beats her heart expand—
As one at each ear and both in a breath
Whispered, "The Great-Duke Ferdinand."

That selfsame instant, underneath,
The Duke rode past in his idle way,
Empty and fine like a swordless sheath.

Gay he rode, with a friend as gay,
Till he threw his head back—"Who is she?"—
"A bride the Riccardi brings home to-day."

ROBERT BROWNING

Hair in heaps lay heavily
Over a pale brow spirit-pure—
Carved like the heart of the coal-black tree,

Crisped like a war steed's enclosure—
And vainly sought to dissemble her eyes
Of the blackest black our eyes endure,

And lo, a blade for a knight's emprise
Filled the fine empty sheath of a man—
The Duke grew straightway brave and wise.

He looked at her as a lover can;
She looked at him, as one who awakes:
The past was a sleep, and her life began.

Now, love so ordered for both their sakes,
A feast was held that selfsame night
In the pile which the mighty shadow makes.

(For Via Larga is three-parts light,
But the palace overshadows one,
Because of a crime, which may God requite!

To Florence and God the wrong was done,
Through the first republic's murder there
By Cosimo and his cursèd son.)

The Duke (with the statue's face in the square)
Turned in the midst of his multitude
At the bright approach of the bridal pair.

Face to face the lovers stood
A single minute and no more
While the bridegroom bent as a man subdued—

Bowed till his bonnet brushed the floor—
For the Duke on the lady a kiss conferred,
As the courtly custom was of yore.

In a minute can lovers exchange a word?
If a word did pass, which I do not think,
Only one out of a thousand heard.

That was the bridegroom. At day's brink
He and his bride were alone at last
In a bed chamber by a taper's blink.

Calmly he said that her lot was cast,
That the door she had passed was shut on her
Till the final catafalk repassed.

The world meanwhile, its noise and stir,
Through a certain window facing the East
She could watch like a convent's chronicler.

Since passing the door might lead to a feast,
And a feast might lead to so much beside,
He, of many evils, chose the least.

"Freely I choose too," said the bride—
"Your window and its world suffice,"
Replied the tongue, while the heart replied—

"If I spend the night with that devil twice,
May his window serve as my loop of hell
Whence a damned soul looks on paradise!

"I fly to the Duke who loves me well,
Sit by his side and laugh at sorrow
Ere I count another ave-bell.

1999

" 'Tis only the coat of a page to borrow,
And tie my hair in a horse-boy's trim,
And I save my soul—but not to-morrow—"

(She checked herself and her eye grew dim)
"My father tarries to bless my state:
I must keep it one day more for him.

"Is one day more so long to wait?
Moreover the Duke rides past, I know;
We shall see each other, sure as fate."

She turned on her side and slept.   Just so!
So we resolve on a thing and sleep:
So did the lady, ages ago.

That night the Duke said, "Dear or cheap
As the cost of this cup of bliss may prove
To body or soul, I will drain it deep."

And on the morrow, bold with love,
He beckoned the bridegroom (close on call,
As his duty bade, by the Duke's alcove)

And smiled " 'Twas a very funeral,
Your lady will think, this feast of ours—
A shame to efface whate'er befall!

"What if we break from the Arno bowers,
And try if Petraja, cool and green,
Cure last night's faults with this morning's flowers?"

The bridegroom, not a thought to be seen
On his steady brow and quiet mouth,
Said, "Too much favor for me so mean!

"But alas! my lady leaves the South;
Each wind that comes from the Apennine
Is a menace to her tender youth:

"Nor a way exists, the wise opine,
If she quits her palace twice this year,
To avert the flower of life's decline."

Quoth the Duke, "A sage and a kindly fear.
Moreover Petraja is cold this spring:
Be our feast to-night as usual here!"

And then to himself—"Which night shall bring
Thy bride to her lover's embraces, fool—
Or I am the fool, and thou art the king!

"Yet my passion must wait a night, nor cool—
For to-night the Envoy arrives from France
Whose heart I unlock with thyself, my tool.

"I need thee still and might miss perchance.
To-day is not wholly lost, beside,
With its hope of my lady's countenance:

"For I ride—what should I do but ride?
And passing her palace, if I list,
May glance at its window—well betide!"

So said, so done: nor the lady missed
One ray that broke from the ardent brow,
Nor a curl of the lips where the spirit kissed.

Be sure that each renewed the vow,
No morrow's sun should arise and set
And leave them then as it left them now.

But next day passed, and next day yet,
With still fresh cause to wait one day more
Ere each leaped over the parapet.

And still, as love's brief morning wore,
With a gentle start, half smile, half sigh,
They found love not as it seemed before.

They thought it would work infallibly,
But not in despite of heaven and earth:
The rose would blow when the storm passed by.

Meantime they could profit in winter's dearth
By store of fruits that supplant the rose:
The world and its ways have a certain worth:

And to press a point while these oppose
Were simple policy, better wait:
We lose no friends and we gain no foes.

Meantime, worse fates than a lover's fate,
Who daily may ride and pass and look
Where his lady watches behind the grate!

And she—she watched the square like a book
Holding one picture and only one,
Which daily to find she undertook:

When the picture was reached the book was done,
And she turned from the picture at night to scheme
Of tearing it out for herself next sun.

So weeks grew months, years; gleam by gleam
The glory dropped from their youth and love,
And both perceived they had dreamed a dream;

Which hovered as dreams do, still above:
But who can take a dream for a truth?
Oh, hide our eyes from the next remove!

One day as the lady saw her youth
Depart, and the silver thread that streaked
Her hair, and, worn by the serpent's tooth,

The brow so puckered, the chin so peaked—
And wondered who the woman was,
Hollow-eyed and haggard-cheeked,

Fronting her silent in the glass—
"Summon here," she suddenly said,
"Before the rest of my old self pass,

"Him, the Carver, a hand to aid,
Who fashions the clay no love will change,
And fixes a beauty never to fade.

"Let Robbia's craft so apt and strange
Arrest the remains of young and fair,
And rivet them while the seasons range.

"Make me a face on the window there,
Waiting as ever, mute the while,
My love to pass below in the square!

"And let me think that it may beguile
Dreary days which the dead must spend
Down in their darkness under the aisle,

"To say, 'What matters it at the end?
I did no more while my heart was warm
Than does that image, my pale-faced friend.'

ROBERT BROWNING

"Where is the use of the lip's red charm,
The heaven of hair, the pride of the brow,
And the blood that blues the inside arm—

"Unless we turn, as the soul knows how,
The earthly gift to an end divine?
A lady of clay is as good, I trow."

But long ere Robbia's cornice, fine,
With flowers and fruits which leaves enlace,
Was set where now is the empty shrine—

(And, leaning out of a bright blue space,
As a ghost might lean from a chink of sky,
The passionate pale lady's face—

Eyeing ever, with earnest eye
And quick-turned neck at its breathless stretch,
Some one who ever is passing by—)

The duke had sighed like the simplest wretch
In Florence, "Youth—my dream escapes!
Will its record stay?" And he bade them fetch

Some subtle moulder of brazen shapes—
"Can the soul, the will, die out of a man
Ere his body find the grave that gapes?

"John of Douay shall effect my plan,
Set me on horseback here aloft,
Alive, as the crafty sculptor can,

"In the very square I have crossed so oft:
That men may admire, when future suns
Shall touch the eyes to a purpose soft,

"While the mouth and the brow stay brave in bronze—
Admire and say, 'When he was alive
How he would take his pleasure once!'

"And it shall go hard but I contrive
To listen the while, and laugh in my tomb
At idleness which aspires to strive."

———————

So! While these wait the trump of doom,
How do their spirits pass, I wonder,
Nights and days in the narrow room?

Still, I suppose, they sit and ponder
What a gift life was, ages ago,
Six steps out of the chapel yonder.

Only they see not God, I know,
Nor all that chivalry of his,
The soldier-saints who, row on row,

Burn upward each to his point of bliss—
Since, the end of life being manifest,
He had burned his way through the world to this.

I hear you reproach, "But delay was best,
For their end was a crime." Oh, a crime will do
As well, I reply, to serve for a test,

As a virtue golden through and through,
Sufficient to vindicate itself
And prove its worth at a moment's view!

Must a game be played for the sake of pelf?
Where a button goes, 'twere an epigram
To offer the stamp of the very Guelph.

The true has no value beyond the sham;
As well the counter as coin, I submit,
When your table's a hat, and your prize, a dram.

Stake your counter as boldly every whit,
Venture as warily, use the same skill,
Do your best, whether winning or losing it,

If you choose to play!—is my principle.
Let a man contend to the uttermost
For his life's set prize, be it what it will!

The counter our lovers staked was lost
As surely as if it were lawful coin;
And the sin I impute to each frustrate ghost

Is—the unlit lamp and the ungirt loin,
Though the end in sight was a vice, I say.
You of the virtue (we issue join)
How strive you? *De te, fabula!*

Soliloquy of the Spanish Cloister

G R-R-R—there go, my heart's abhorrence!
  Water your damned flower-pots, do!
If hate killed men, Brother Lawrence,
  God's blood, would not mine kill you!
What? your myrtle-bush wants trimming?
  Oh, that rose has prior claims—
Needs its leaden vase filled brimming?
  Hell dry you up with its flames!

2006

At the meal we sit together:
  Salve tibi! I must hear
Wise talk of the kind of weather,
  Sort of season, time of year:
Not a plenteous cork-crop: scarcely
  Dare we hope oak-galls, I doubt:
What's the Latin name for "parsley"?
  What's the Greek name for Swine's Snout?

Whew! We'll have our platter burnished,
  Laid with care on our own shelf!
With a fire-new spoon we're furnished,
  And a goblet for ourself,
Rinsed like something sacrificial
  Ere 't is fit to touch our chaps—
Marked with L. for our initial!
  (He-he! There his lily snaps!)

Saint, forsooth! While brown Dolores
  Squats outside the Convent bank
With Sanchicha, telling stories,
  Steeping tresses in the tank,
Blue-black, lustrous, thick like horsehairs—
  Can't I see his dead eye glow,
Bright as 't were a Barbary corsair's?
  (That is, if he'd let it show!)

When he finishes refection,
  Knife and fork he never lays
Cross-wise, to my recollection,
  As do I, in Jesu's praise.
I the Trinity illustrate,
  Drinking watered orange-pulp—
In three sips the Arian frustrate;
  While he drains his at one gulp.

Oh, those melons? If he's able
   We're to have a feast; so nice!
One goes to the Abbot's table,
   All of us get each a slice.
How go on your flowers? None double?
   Not one fruit-sort can you spy?
Strange!—And I, too, at such trouble
   Keep them close-nipped on the sly!

There's a great text in Galatians,
   Once you trip on it, entails
Twenty-nine distinct damnations,
   One sure, if another fails:
If I trip him just a-dying,
   Sure of heaven as sure can be,
Spin him round and send him flying
   Off to hell, a Manichee?

Or, my scrofulous French novel
   On grey paper with blunt type!
Simply glance at it, you grovel
   Hand and foot in Belial's gripe:
If I double down its pages
   At the woeful sixteenth print,
When he gathers his greengages,
   Ope a sieve and slip it in 't?

Or, there's Satan!—one might venture
   Pledge one's soul to him, yet leave
Such a flaw in the indenture
   As he'd miss till, past retrieve,
Blasted lay that rose-acacia
   We're so proud of! *Hy, Zy, Hine*
'St, there's Vespers! *Plena gratiâ*
   Ave, Virgo! Gr-r-r—you swine!

ROBERT BROWNING

One Word More

*This poem was originally appended to the collection en-
titled "Men and Women"—a dedication to Mrs. Browning.
The volume was in one sense a return for her "Sonnets
from the Portuguese." Browning explains why he has de-
sired to give something of his best, some gift which is not
a gift to the world but to the woman he loves; and as the
meanest of God's creatures—*

> *"Boasts two soul-sides: one to face the world with;
> One to show a woman when he loves her!"*

*Artist and artisan alike are powerfully moved on occasion
to do something worthy to present to the loved one.
Raphael, not content with painting, must pour out his soul
in poetry for the woman of his heart (did she love the
volume of a hundred sonnets all her life?) and Browning
says he and his poet-wife would rather read that volume
than wonder at the Madonnas which have immortalized
Raphael. No artist lives and loves who desires not for
once and for one to express himself in a language natural
to him and the occasion, but which to others is but an art.
And so the painter will forego his painting and write a
poem, the writer will try to paint a picture "once and for
one only"—*

> *"So to be the man and leave the artist."*

I

THERE they are, my fifty men and women
   Naming me the fifty poems finished!
Take them, Love, the book and me together:
Where the heart lies, let the brain lie also.

II

Rafael made a century of sonnets,
Made and wrote them in a certain volume
Dinted with the silver-pointed pencil
Else he only used to draw Madonnas:
These, the world might view—but one, the volume.
Who that one, you ask? Your heart instructs you.
Did she live and love it all her lifetime?
Did she drop, his lady of the sonnets,
Die, and let it drop beside her pillow
Where it lay in place of Rafael's glory,
Rafael's cheek so duteous and so loving,
Cheek, the world was wont to hail a painter's,
Rafael's cheek, her love had turned a poet's?

III

You and I would rather read that volume,
(Taken to his beating bosom by it)
Lean and list the bosom-beats of Rafael,
Would we not? than wonder at Madonnas—
Her, San Sisto names, and Her, Foligno,
Her, that visits Florence in a vision,
Her, that's left with lilies in the Louvre—
Seen by us and all the world in circle.

IV

You and I will never read that volume.
Guido Reni, like his own eye's apple
Guarded long the treasure-book and loved it.
Guido Reni dying, all Bologna
Cried, and the world cried too, "Ours, the treasure!"
Suddenly, as rare things will, it vanished.

V

Dante once prepared to paint an angel:
Whom to please? You whisper "Beatrice."
While he mused and traced it and retraced it,
(Peradventure with a pen corroded
Still by drops of that hot ink he dipped for,
When, his left-hand i' the hair o' the wicked,
Back he held the brow and pricked its stigma,
Bit into the live man's flesh for parchment,
Loosed him, laughed to see the writing rankle,
Let the wretch go festering through Florence)
Dante, who loved well because he hated,
Hated wickedness that hinders loving,
Dante standing, studying his angel—
In there broke the folk of his Inferno.
Says he—"Certain people of importance"
(Such he gave his daily dreadful line to)
"Entered and would seize, forsooth, the poet."
Says the poet—"Then I stopped my painting."

VI

You and I would rather see that angel,
Painted by the tenderness of Dante,
Would we not?—than read a fresh Inferno.

VII

You and I will never see that picture.
While he mused on love and Beatrice,
While he softened o'er his outlined angel,
In they broke, those "people of importance:"
We and Bice bear the loss forever.

VIII

What of Rafael's sonnets, Dante's picture?
This: no artist lives and loves, that longs not
Once, and only once, and for one only,
(Ah, the prize!) to find his love a language
Fit and fair and simple and sufficient—
Using nature that's an art to others,
Not, this one time, art that's turned his nature.
Ay, of all the artists living, loving,
None but would forego his proper dowry—
Does he paint? he fain would write a poem—
Does he write? he fain would paint a picture,
Put to proof art alien to the artist's,
Once, and only once, and for one only,
So to be the man and leave the artist,
Gain the man's joy, miss the artist's sorrow.

IX

Wherefore? Heaven's gift takes earth's abatement!
He who smites the rock and spreads the water,
Bidding drink and live a crowd beneath him,
Even he, the minute makes immortal,
Proves, perchance, but mortal in the minute.
Desecrates, belike, the deed in doing.
While he smites, how can he but remember,
So he smote before, in such a peril,
When they stood and mocked—"Shall smiting help us?"
When they drank and sneered—"A stroke is easy!"
When they wiped their mouths and went their journey,
Throwing him for thanks—"But drought was pleasant."
Thus old memories mar the actual triumph;
Thus the doing savors of disrelish;
Thus achievement lacks a gracious somewhat;

O'er-importuned brows becloud the mandate,
Carelessness or consciousness—the gesture.
For he bears an ancient wrong about him,
Sees and knows again those phalanxed faces,
Hears, yet one time more, the 'customed prelude—
"How shouldst thou, of all men, smite, and save us?"
Guesses what is like to prove the sequel—
"Egypt's flesh-pots—nay, the drought was better."

X

Oh, the crowd must have emphatic warrant!
Theirs, the Sinai-forehead's cloven brilliance,
Right-arm's rod-sweep, tongue's imperial fiat.
Never dares the man put off the prophet.

XI

Did he love one face from out the thousands,
(Were she Jethro's daughter, white and wifely,
Were she but the Æthiopian bondslave)
He would envy yon dumb patient camel,
Keeping a reserve of scanty water
Meant to save his own life in the desert;
Ready in the desert to deliver
(Kneeling down to let his breast be opened)
Hoard and life together for his mistress.

XII

I shall never, in the years remaining,
Paint you pictures, no, nor carve you statues,
Make you music that should all-express me;
So it seems: I stand on my attainment.
This of verse alone, one life allows me;
Verse and nothing else have I to give you.

Other heights in other lives, God willing:
All the gifts from all the heights, your own, Love!

XIII

Yet a semblance of resource avails us—
Shade so finely touched, love's sense must seize it.
Take these lines, look lovingly and nearly,
Lines I write the first time and the last time.
He who works in fresco, steals a hair-brush,
Curbs the liberal hand, subservient proudly,
Cramps his spirit, crowds its all in little,
Makes a strange art of an art familiar,
Fills his lady's missal-marge with flowerets.
He who blows through bronze, may breathe through silver,
Fitly serenade a slumbrous princess.
He who writes, may write for once as I do.

XIV

Love, you saw me gather men and women,
Live or dead or fashioned by my fancy,
Enter each and all, and use their service,
Speak from every mouth—the speech, a poem.
Hardly shall I tell my joys and sorrows,
Hope and fears, belief and disbelieving:
I am mine and yours—the rest be all men's,
Karshish, Cleon, Norbert, and the fifty.
Let me speak this once in my true person,
Not as Lippo, Roland, or Andrea,
Though the fruit of speech be just this sentence:
Pray you, look on these my men and women,
Take and keep my fifty poems finished;
Where my heart lies, let my brain lie also!
Poor the speech; be how I speak, for all things.

XV

Not but that you know me! Lo, the moon's self!
Here in London, yonder late in Florence,
Still we find her face, the thrice-transfigured,
Curving on a sky imbrued with color,
Drifted over Fiesole by twilight,
Came she, our new crescent of a hair's-breadth.
Full she flared it, lamping Samminiato,
Rounder 'twixt the cypresses, and rounder,
Perfect till the nightingales applauded.
Now, a piece of her old self, impoverished,
Hard to greet, she traverses the house-roofs,
Hurries with unhandsome thrift of silver,
Goes dispiritedly, glad to finish.

XVI

What, there's nothing in the moon noteworthy?
Nay: for if that moon could love a mortal,
Use, to charm him (so to fit a fancy)
All her magic ('tis the old sweet mythos)
She would turn a new side to her mortal,
Side unseen of herdsman, huntsman, steersman—
Blank to Zoroaster on his terrace,
Blind to Galileo on his turret,
Dumb to Homer, dumb to Keats—him, even!
Think, the wonder of the moonstruck mortal—
When she turns round, comes again in heaven,
Opens out anew for worse or better!
Proves she like some portent of an iceberg
Swimming full upon the ship it founders,
Hungry with huge teeth of splintered crystals?
Proves she as the paved work of a sapphire
Seen by Moses when he climbed the mountain?

Moses, Aaron, Nadab and Abihu
Climbed and saw the very God, the Highest,
Stand upon the paved work of a sapphire.
Like the bodied heaven in his clearness
Shone the stone, the sapphire of that paved work,
When they ate and drank and saw God also!

XVII

What were seen? None knows, none ever shall know.
Only this is sure—the sight were other,
Not the moon's same side, born late in Florence,
Dying now impoverished here in London.
God be thanked, the meanest of his creatures
Boasts two soul-sides, one to face the world with,
One to show a woman when he loves her.

XVIII

This I say of me, but think of you, Love!
This to you—yourself my moon of poets!
Ah, but that's the world's side, there's the wonder,
Thus they see you, praise you, think they know you!
There, in turn I stand with them and praise you—
Out of my own self, I dare to phrase it.
But the best is when I glide from out them,
Cross a step or two of dubious twilight,
Come out on the other side, the novel
Silent silver lights and darks undreamed of,
Where I hush and bless myself with silence.

XIX

Oh, their Rafael of the dear Madonnas,
Oh, their Dante of the dread Inferno,
Wrote one song—and in my brain I sing it,
Drew one angel—borne, see, on my bosom!

ROBERT BROWNING

Prospice

FEAR death?—to feel the fog in my throat,
　　The mist in my face,
When the snows begin, and the blasts denote
　　I am nearing the place,
The power of the night, the press of the storm,
　　The post of the foe;
Where he stands, the Arch Fear in a visible form,
　　Yet the strong man must go:
For the journey is done and the summit attained,
　　And the barriers fall,
Though a battle's to fight ere the guerdon be gained,
　　The reward of it all.
I was ever a fighter, so—one fight more,
　　The best and the last!
I would hate that death bandaged my eyes, and forbore
　　And bade me creep past.
No! let me taste the whole of it, fare like my peers
　　The heroes of old,
Bear the brunt, in a minute pay glad life's arrears
　　Of pain, darkness and cold.
For sudden the worst turns the best to the brave,
　　The black minute's at end,
And the elements' rage, the fiend-voices that rave,
　　Shall dwindle, shall blend,
Shall change, shall become first a peace out of pain,
　　Then a light, then thy breast,
O thou soul of my soul! I shall clasp thee again,
　　And with God be the rest!

Epilogue

AT the midnight in the silence of the sleep-time,
    When you set your fancies free,
Will they pass to where—by death, fools think, imprisoned—
Low he lies who once so loved you, whom ye loved so—
      Pity me?

Oh to love so, be so loved, yet so mistaken!
    What had I on earth to do
With the slothful, with the mawkish, the unmanly?
Like the aimless, helpless, hopeless, did I drivel—
      Being—who?

One who never turned his back but marched breast forward,
    Never doubted clouds would break,
Never dreamed, though right were worsted, wrong would triumph,
Held we fall to rise, are baffled to fight better,
      Sleep to wake.

No, at noonday in the bustle of man's work-time
    Greet the unseen with a cheer!
Bid him forward, breast and back as either should be,
"Strive and thrive!" cry "Speed—fight on, fare ever
      There as here!"

WILLIAM BELL SCOTT
SCOTLAND, 1812—1890

The Witch's Ballad

O I hae come from far away,
　　From a warm land far away,
A southern land across the sea,
With sailor-lads about the mast,
Merry and canny, and kind to me.

And I hae been to yon town
　　To try my luck in yon town;
Nort, and Mysie, Elspie too.
Right braw we were to pass the gate,
Wi' gowden clasps on girdles blue.

Mysie smiled wi' miminy [1] mouth,
　　Innocent mouth, miminy mouth:
Elspie wore a scarlet gown,
Nort's grey eyes were unco' gleg [2]
My Castile comb was like a crown.

We walked abreast all up the street,
　　Into the market up the street;
Our hair with marigolds was wound,
Our bodices with love-knots laced,
Our merchandise with tansy bound.

[1] miminy] prim, demure.
[2] gleg] bright, sharp.

WILLIAM BELL SCOTT

Nort had chickens, I had cocks,
   Gamesome cocks, loud-crowing cocks:
Mysie ducks, and Elspie drakes—
For a wee groat or a pound:
We lost nae time wi' gives and takes.

Lost nae time, for well we knew,
   In our sleeves full well we knew,
When the gloaming came that night,
Duck nor drake, nor hen nor cock
Would be found by candle-light.

And when our chaffering all was done,
   All was paid for, sold and done,
We drew a glove on ilka hand,
We sweetly curtsied, each to each,
And deftly danced a saraband.

The market-lassies looked and laughed,
   Left their gear, and looked and laughed;
They made as they would join the game,
But soon their mithers, wild and wud,[1]
With whack and screech they stopped the same.

Sae loud the tongues o' randies[2] grew,
   The flytin'[3] and the skirlin'[4] grew,
At all the windows in the place,
Wi' spoons or knives, wi' needle or awl,
Was thrust out every hand and face.

[1] wud] mad.
[2] randies] viragoes.
[3] flytin'] scolding.
[4] skirlin'] shrieking.

And down each stair they thronged anon
  Gentle, semple, thronged anon;
Souter [1] and tailor, frowsy Nan,
The ancient widow young again,
Simpering behind her fan.

Without a choice, against their will,
  Doited,[2] dazed, against their will,
The market lassie and her mither,
The farmer and his husbandman,
Hand in hand dance a' thegither.

Slow at first, but faster soon,
  Still increasing, wild and fast,
Hoods and mantles, hats and hose,
Blindly doffed and cast away,
Left them naked, heads and toes.

They would have torn us limb from limb,
  Dainty limb from dainty limb;
But never one of them could win
Across the line that I had drawn
With bleeding thumb a-widdershin.[3]

But there was Jeff the provost's son,
  Jeff the provost's only son;
There was Father Auld himsel',
The Lombard frae the hostelry,
And the lawyer Peter Fell.

[1] souter] cobbler.
[2] doited] mazed.
[3] a-widdershin] the wrong way of the sun: or E. to W. through N.

All goodly men we singled out,
  Waled[1] them well, and singled out,
And drew them by the left hand in;
Mysie the priest, and Elspie won
The Lombard, Nort the lawyer carle,
I mysel' the provost's son.

Then, with cantrip[2] kisses seven,
  Three times round with kisses seven,
Warped and woven there spun we
Arms and legs and flaming hair,
Like a whirlwind on the sea.

Like a wind that sucks the sea,
  Over and in and on the sea,
Good sooth it was a mad delight;
And every man of all the four
Shut his eyes and laughed outright.

Laughed as long as they had breath,
  Laughed while they had sense or breath;
And close about us coiled a mist
Of gnats and midges, wasps and flies,
Like the whirlwind shaft it rist.

Drawn up I was right off my feet,
  Into the mist and off my feet;
And, dancing on each chimney-top,
I saw a thousand darling imps
Keeping time with skip and hop.

[1] waled] chose.
[2] cantrip] magic.

And on the provost's brave ridge-tile,
  On the provost's grand ridge-tile,
The Blackamoor first to master me
I saw, I saw that winsome smile,
The mouth that did my heart beguile,
And spoke the great Word over me,
In the land beyond the sea.

I called his name, I called aloud,
  Alas! I called on him aloud;
And then he filled his hand with stour,[1]
And threw it towards me in the air;
My mouse flew out, I lost my power!

My lusty strength and power were gone;
  Power was gone, and all was gone.
He will not let me love him more!
Of bell and whip and horse's tail
He cares not if I find a store.

But I am proud if he is fierce!
  I am as proud as he is fierce:
I'll turn about and backward go,
If I meet again that Blackamoor,
And he'll help us then, for he shall know
I seek another paramour.

And we'll gang once more to yon town,
  Wi' better luck to yon town;
We'll walk in silk and cramoisie,[2]
And I shall wed the provost's son
My lady of the town I'll be!

[1] stour] dust.
[2] cramoisie] crimson.

WILLIAM BELL SCOTT

For I was born a crowned king's child,
  Born and nursed a king's child,
King o' a land ayont[1] the sea,
Where the Blackamoor kissed me first,
And taught me art and glamourie.[2]

Each one in her wame shall hide
  Her hairy mouse, her wary mouse,
Fed on madwort and agramie—
Wear amber beads between her breasts,
And blind-worm's skin about her knee.

The Lombard shall be Elspie's man,
  Elspie's gowden husband-man;
Nort shall take the lawyer's hand;
The priest shall swear another vow:
We'll dance again the saraband!

[1] ayont] beyond.
[2] glamourie] wizardry.

FREDERICK W. FABER
ENGLAND, 1814–1863

Aged Cities

I HAVE known cities with the strong-armed Rhine
   Clasping their moldered quays in lordly sweep;
And lingered where the Main's low waters shine
Through Tyrian Frankfort; and been fain to weep
'Mid the green cliffs where pale Mosella laves
That Roman sepulchre, imperial Treves.
Ghent boasts her street, and Bruges her moonlight
   square;
And holy Mechlin, Rome or Flanders, stands,
Like a queen-mother, on her spacious lands;
And Antwerp shoots her glowing spire in air.
Yet have I seen no place, by inland brook,
Hill-top, or plain, or trim arcaded bowers,
That carries age so nobly in its look,
As Oxford with the sun upon her towers.

CHARLES MACKAY
SCOTLAND, 1814—1889

Tubal Cain

OLD Tubal Cain was a man of might
   In the days when Earth was young:
By the fierce red light of his furnace bright
   The strokes of his hammer rung;
And he lifted high his brawny hand
   On the iron glowing clear,
Till the sparks rushed out in scarlet showers,
   As he fashioned the sword and spear.
And he sang: "Hurra for my handiwork!
   Hurra for the spear and sword!
Hurra for the hand that shall wield them well,
   For he shall be king and lord! "

To Tubal Cain came many a one,
   As he wrought by his roaring fire,
And each one prayed for a strong steel blade
   As the crown of his desire;
And he made them weapons sharp and strong,
   Till they shouted loud for glee,
And gave him gifts of pearl and gold,
   And spoils of the forest free.
And they sang "Hurra for Tubal Cain,
   Who has given us strength anew!
Hurra for the smith, hurra for the fire,
   And hurra for the metal true!"

But a sudden change came over his heart
  Ere the setting of the sun,
And Tubal Cain was filled with pain
  For the evil he had done;
He saw that men, with rage and hate,
  Made war upon their kind,
That land was red with the blood they shed,
  In their lust for carnage blind.
And he said: "Alas! that ever I made,
  Or that skill of mine should plan,
The spear and the sword for men whose joy
  Is to slay their fellow-man!"

And for many a day old Tubal Cain
  Sat brooding over his woe;
And his hand forebore to smite the ore,
  And his furnace smoldered low.
But he rose at last with a cheerful face,
  And a bright courageous eye,
And bared his strong right arm for work,
  While the quick flames mounted high.
And he sang: "Hurra for my handiwork!"
  And the red sparks lit the air;
"Not alone for the blade was the bright steel made,"
  And he fashioned the first ploughshare.

The Children's Auction

WHO bids for the little children—
    Body and soul and brain?
Who bids for the little children—
    Young and without a stain?
"Will no one bid," said England,
    "For their souls so pure and white,
And fit for all good or evil
    The world on their page may write?"

"We bid," said Pest and Famine;
    "We bid for life and limb;
Fever and pain and squalor,
    Their bright young eyes shall dim.
When the children grow too many,
    We'll nurse them as our own,
And hide them in secret places
    Where none may hear their moan."

"I bid," said Beggary, howling;
    "I bid for them one and all!
I'll teach them a thousand lessons—
    To lie, to skulk, to crawl!
They shall sleep in my lair like maggots,
    They shall rot in the fair sunshine;
And if they serve my purpose
    I hope they'll answer thine."

"I'll bid you higher and higher,"
    Said Crime, with a wolfish grin;
"For I love to lead the children
    Through the pleasant paths of sin.

CHARLES MACKAY

They shall swarm in the streets to pilfer,
 They shall plague the broad highway,
They shall grow too old for pity
 And ripe for the law to slay.

"Give me the little children,
 Ye good, ye rich, ye wise,
And let the busy world spin round
 While ye shut your idle eyes;
And your judges shall have work,
 And your lawyers wag the tongue,
And the jailers and policemen
 Shall be fathers to the young!"

AUBREY DE VERE
Ireland, 1814–1902

The Sun-God

I SAW the Master of the Sun. He stood
 High in his luminous car, himself more bright;
An archer of immeasurable might;
On his left shoulder hung his quivered load;
Spurned by his steeds the eastern mountains glowed;
Forward his eagle eye and bow of Light
He bent, and while both hands that arched embowed,
Shaft after Shaft pursued the flying night.
No wings profaned that god-like form; around
His neck high-held an ever-moving crowd
Of locks hung glistening: while such perfect sound
Fell from his bowstring that the ethereal dome
Thrilled as a dewdrop; and each passing cloud
Expanded, whitening like the ocean foam.

AUBREY DE VERE

The Divine Presence

Reverence and awe—essential characteristics of the devotional spirit—are strongly marked in this poet; and short as some of his religious poems are, they seem to reproduce the very atmosphere of devotion from which they evidently sprung. Take, for example, the lines that follow.

ALL but unutterable Name!
  Adorable, yet awful sound!
Thee can the sinful nations frame
  Save with their foreheads on the ground?

Soul-searching and all-cleansing Fire;
  To see Thy countenance were to die:
Yet how beyond the bound retire
  Of Thy serene immensity?

Thou mov'st beside us, if the spot
  We change—a noteless, wandering tribe;
The orbits of our life and thought
  In Thee their little arcs describe.

In the dead calm, at cool of day,
  We hear Thy voice, and turn, and flee:
Thy love outstrips us on our way!
  From Thee, O God, we fly—to Thee.

Lines

The sights o'er yonder snowy range
  Shine yet intense, and tender;
Or, slowly passing, only change
  From splendor on to splendor.

AUBREY DE VERE

Before the dying eyes of day
    Immortal visions wander;
Dreams prescient of a purer ray,
    And morn spread still beyond her.

Lo! heavenward now those gleams expire,
    In heavenly melancholy,
The barrier-mountain, peak and spire,
    Relinquishing them slowly.

Thus shine, O God! our mortal powers,
    While grief and joy refine them—
And when in death they fade, be ours
    Thus gently to resign them!

CHARLES HEAVYSEGE
ENGLAND, 1816-?

HEAVYSEGE is another illustration of struggling and
defeated genius. In 1853 he emigrated to Canada
where he found employment in a machine shop. Saul as
an epical subject had haunted his mind for years; and
finally *Saul, a Drama,* saw the light of print in 1857.
While the general reception of it was depressing, yet
Nathaniel Hawthorne—then in Liverpool—secured a
critique of it in *The North British Review.* The drama
has serious artistic faults, yet it carries a fine flavor of
the Elizabethan Age, and it is sprinkled here and there
with quaint and original images. I give two selections
which will doubtless be new to many readers.

Saul's Faithfulness

THE winds of Heaven
    Behind thee blow: and on our enemies' eyes,
May the sun smite to-morrow, and blind them for thee!
But, O Saul, do not fail us.
   SAUL.   Fail ye?
Let the morn fail to break; I will not break
My word. Haste, or I'm there before you;
But, swift and silent as the streaming wind,
Unseen approach, then, gathering up my force
At dawning, sweep on Ammon, as Night's blast
Sweeps down from Carmel on the dusky sea.

Hell's Road

FIRST DEMON. Now let us down to Hell: we've
    seen the last.
SECOND DEMON. Stay; for the road thereto is yet in-
cumbered
With the descending spectres of the killed.
'Tis said they choke Hell's gates, and stretch from
    thence
Out like a tongue upon the silent gulf;
Wherein our spirits—even as terrestrial ships
That are detained by foul winds in an offing—
Linger perforce, and feel broad gusts of sighs
That swing them on the dark and billowless waste,
O'er which come sounds more dismal than the boom,
At midnight of the salt flood's foaming surf—
Even dead Amalek's moan and lamentation.

PHILIP JAMES BAILEY
ENGLAND, 1816-1902

Lucifer's Song

FROM "FESTUS"

THOU hast more music in thy voice
  Than to the spheres is given,
And more temptations on thy lips
  Than lost the angels Heaven.
Thou hast more brightness in thine eyes
  Than all the stars which burn,
More dazzling art thou than the throne
  We fallen dared to spurn.

Go, search through Heaven—the sweetest smile
  That lightens there is thine;
And through Hell's burning darkness breaks
  No frown so fell as mine.
One smile—'twill light, one tear—'twill cool:
  These will be more to me
Than all the wealth of all the worlds,
  Or boundless power could be.

We Live in Deeds

WE live in deeds, not years; in thoughts, not
    breaths;
In feelings, not in figures on a dial.
We should count time by heart-throbs. He most lives
Who thinks most, feels the noblest, acts the best.

TOM TAYLOR

ENGLAND, 1817-1880

Tom Taylor of *"Punch,"* England's great humorous paper, which had caricatured Lincoln in the past, made this apology after the assassination.

From *"Abraham Lincoln"*

YOU lay a wreath on murdered Lincoln's bier,
  You, who with mocking pencil wont to trace,
Broad for the self-complacent British sneer,
  His length of shambling limb, his furrowed face,

His gaunt, gnarled hands, his unkempt, bristling hair,
  His garb uncouth, his bearing ill at ease,
His lack of all we prize as debonair,
  Of power or will to shine, of art to please.

You, whose smart pen backed up the pencil's laugh,
  Judging each step as though the way were plain,
Reckless, so it could point its paragraph,
  Of chief's perplexity, or people's pain.

Beside this corpse, that bears for winding-sheet
  The Stars and Stripes he lived to rear anew,
Between the mourners at his head and feet,
  Say, scurrile jester, is there room for *you?*

Yes, he had lived to shame me from my sneer,
  To lame my pencil and confute my pen;
To make me own this hind of princes peer,
  This rail-splitter a true-born king of men.

TOM TAYLOR

My shallow judgment I had learned to rue,
  Noting how to occasion's height he rose;
How his quaint wit made home-truth seem more true;
  How, iron-like, his temper grew by blows:

How humble, yet how hopeful he could be;
  How, in good fortune and in ill, the same;
Nor bitter in success, nor boastful he,
  Thirsty for gold, nor feverish for fame.

He went about his work—such work as few
  Ever had laid on head and heart and hand—
As one who knows, where there's a task to do,
  Man's honest will must Heaven's good grace command;

Who trusts the strength will with the burden grow,
  That God makes instruments to work his will,
If but that will we can arrive to know,
  Nor tamper with the weights of good and ill.

So he went forth to battle, on the side
  That he felt clear was Liberty's and Right's,
As in his peasant boyhood he had plied
  His warfare with rude Nature's thwarting mights. . . .

So he grew up, a destined work to do,
  And lived to do it; four long-suffering years'
Ill-fate, ill-feeling, ill-report lived through,
  And then he heard the hisses changed to cheers,

The taunts to tribute, the abuse to praise,
  And took both with the same unwavering mood—
Till, as he came on light from darkling days,
  And seemed to touch the goal from where he stood,

A felon hand, between the goal and him,
    Reached from behind his back, a trigger prest,
And those perplexed and patient eyes were dim,
    Those gaunt, long-laboring limbs were laid to rest. . . .

EMILY BRONTË
ENGLAND, 1818-1848

THE poetry of Emily Brontë is small in extent and conventional in form. Its burning thoughts are concealed for the most part in the tame and ambling measures dedicated to female verse by the practice of Felicia Hemans and Letitia Landon in England. Finest among her poems is *Last Lines*, that outburst of abiding faith that was found by her sister Charlotte on her desk when she died—a "last poem," says Edmund Gosse, "not to be surpassed in dignity and self-reliance by any in the language." Breathing into her poetry only her insurgent self, she expresses that self so nobly that in some of her verses may be discerned a militant character, which, under other circumstances, might have turned her into a Maid of Orleans or a Madame Roland.

Remembrance

COLD in earth, and the deep snow piled above thee,
    Far, far removed, cold in the dreary grave!
Have I forgot, my only Love, to love thee,
    Severed at last by time's all-severing wave?

Now, when alone, do my thoughts no longer hover
    Over the mountains on that northern shore,

Resting their wings where heath and fern-leaves cover
  Thy noble heart forever, evermore?

Cold in the earth—and fifteen wild Decembers
  From those brown hills have melted into spring;
Faithful, indeed, is the spirit that remembers
  After such years of change and suffering.

Sweet love of youth, forgive, if I forget thee
  While the world's tide is bearing me along;
Other desires and other hopes beset me,
  Hopes which obscure, but cannot do thee wrong.

No later light has lightened up my heaven,
  No second morn has ever shone for me;
All my life's bliss from thy dear life was given;
  All my life's bliss is in the grave with thee.

But when the days of golden dreams had perished,
  And even despair was powerless to destroy;
Then did I learn existence could be cherished,
  Strengthened and fed without the aid of joy.

Then did I check the tears of useless passion,
  Weaned my young soul from yearning after thine;
Sternly denied its burning wish to hasten
  Down to that tomb already more than mine.

And even yet I dare not let it languish,
  Dare not indulge in memory's rapturous pain;
Once drinking deep of that divinest anguish,
  How could I seek the empty world again?

EMILY BRONTE

Last Lines

NO coward soul is mine,
  No trembler in the world's storm-troubled sphere:
I see Heaven's glories shine,
And faith shines equal, arming me from fear,

O God within my breast,
Almighty, ever-present Deity!
  Life—that in me has rest,
As I—undying Life—have power in Thee!

Vain are the thousand creeds
That move men's hearts: unutterably vain;
  Worthless as withered weeds,
Or idlest froth amid the boundless main,

To waken doubt in one
Holding so fast by Thine infinity;
  So surely anchored on
The steadfast rock of immortality.

With wide-embracing love
Thy Spirit animates eternal years,
  Pervades and broods above,
Changes, sustains, dissolves, creates and rears.

Though earth and man were gone,
And suns and universes cease to be,
  And Thou were left alone,
Every existence would exist in Thee.

There is not room for Death,
No atom that his might could render void:
Thou—Thou art Being and Breath,
And what Thou art may never be destroyed.

ELIZA COOK
ENGLAND, 1818-1889

Hang Up His Harp; He'll Wake no More!

HIS young bride stood beside his bed,
  Her weeping watch to keep:
Hush! hush! he stirred not—was he dead,
  Or did he only sleep?

His brow was calm, no change was there,
  No sigh had filled his breath;
Oh, did he wear that smile so fair
  In slumber or in death?

"Reach down his harp," she wildly cried,
  "And if one spark remain,
Let him but hear 'Loch Erroch's Side';
  He'll kindle at the strain.

"That tune ever held his soul in thrall;
  It never breathed in vain;
He'll waken as its echoes fall,
  Or never wake again."

The strings were swept. 'Twas sad to hear
  Sweet music floating there;
For every note called forth a tear
  Of anguish and despair.

"See! see!" she cried, "the tune is o'er:
  No opening eye, no breath;
Hang up his harp; he'll wake no more;
  He sleeps the sleep of death."

ARTHUR HUGH CLOUGH
ENGLAND, 1819-1861

Say Not the Struggle Naught Availeth

SAY not, the struggle naught availeth,
  The labor and the wounds are vain,
The enemy faints not, nor faileth,
  And as things have been they remain.

If hopes were dupes, fears may be liars;
  It may be, in yon smoke concealed,
Your comrades chase even now the fliers,
  And, but for you, possess the field.

For while the tired waves, vainly breaking,
  Seem here no painful inch to gain,
Far back, through creeks and inlets making,
  Comes silent, flooding in, the main.

And not by eastern windows only,
  When daylight comes, comes in the light:
In front, the sun climbs slow, how slowly,
  But westward, look, the land is bright.

ARTHUR HUGH CLOUGH

Where Lies the Land to Which the Ship Would Go?

WHERE lies the land to which the ship would go?
Far, far ahead, is all her seamen know.
And where the land she travels from? Away,
Far, far behind, is all that they can say.

On sunny noons upon the deck's smooth face,
Linked arm in arm how pleasant here to pace;
Or, over the stern reclining, watch below
The foaming wake far widening as we go.

On stormy nights when wild north-westers rave,
How proud a thing to fight with wind and wave!
The dripping sailor on the reeling mast
Exults to bear, and scorns to wish it past.

Where lies the land to which the ship would go?
Far, far ahead, is all her seamen know.
And where the land she travels from? Away,
Far, far behind, is all that they can say.

"With Whom Is No Variableness, Neither Shadow of Turning"

IT fortifies my soul to know
That, though I perish, Truth is so:
That, howsoever I stray and range,
Whate'er I do, Thou dost not change.
I steadier step when I recall
That, if I slip, Thou dost not fall.

ARTHUR HUGH CLOUGH

From "Dipsychus"

"THERE is no God," the wicked saith,
  "And truly it's a blessing,
For what He might have done with us
  It's better only guessing."

"There is no God," a youngster thinks,
  "Or really, if there may be,
He surely did not mean a man
  Always to be a baby."

"There is no God, or if there is,"
  The tradesman thinks, " 'twere funny
If He should take it ill in me
  To make a little money."

"Whether there be," the rich man says,
  "It matters very little,
For I and mine, thank somebody,
  Are not in want of victual."

Some others, also, to themselves,
  Who scarce so much as doubt it,
Think there is none, when they are well
  And do not think about it.

But country folks who live beneath
  The shadow of the steeple;
The parson and the parson's wife,
  And mostly married people;

Youths green and happy in first love,
    So thankful for illusion;
And men caught out in what the world
    Calls guilt, in first confusion;

And almost every one when age,
    Disease, or sorrows strike him,
Inclines to think there is a God,
    Or something very like Him.

Easter Day

NAPLES, 1849

I

THROUGH the great sinful streets of Naples as I
        passed,
    With fiercer heat than flamed above my head
My heart was hot within me; till at last
    My brain was lightened when my tongue had said—
            Christ is not risen!
            Christ is not risen, no—
                He lies and molders low;
            Christ is not risen!

What though the stone were rolled away, and though
        The grave found empty there?—
        If not there, then elsewhere;
If not where Joseph laid Him first, why then
        Where other men
Translaid Him after, in some humbler clay,
        Long ere to-day
Corruption that sad perfect work hath done,
Which here she scarcely, lightly had begun:

ARTHUR HUGH CLOUGH

The foul engendered worm
Feeds on the flesh of the life-giving **form**
Of our most Holy and Anointed One.
He is not risen, no—
He lies and molders low;
Christ is not risen!

What if the women, ere the dawn was gray,
Saw one or more great angels, as they say
(Angels, or Him Himself)? Yet neither there, **nor**
then,
Nor afterwards, nor elsewhere, nor at all,
Hath He appeared to Peter or the Ten;
Nor save in thunderous terror, to blind Saul;
Save in an after Gospel and late Creed,
He is not risen, indeed—
Christ is not risen!

Or, what if even, as runs a tale, the **Ten**
Saw, heard, and touched, again and yet again?
What if at Emmaüs' inn, and by Capernaum's Lake,
Came One, the bread that brake—
Came One that spake as never mortal spake,
And with them ate, and drank, and stood, and walked
about?
Ah? "some" did well to "doubt!"
Ah! the true Christ, while these things came to pass,
Nor heard, nor spake, nor walked, nor lived, alas!
He was not risen, no—
He lay and moldered low,
Christ was not risen!

2044

As circulates in some great city crowd
A rumor changeful, vague, importunate and loud,
From no determined centre or of fact
      Or authorship exact,
     Which no man can deny
       Nor verify;
     So spread the wondrous fame;
     He all the same
     Lay senseless, moldering, low:
     He was not risen, no—
       Christ was not risen!

Ashes to ashes, dust to dust;
As of the unjust, also of the just—
   Yea, of that Just One, too!
This is the one sad Gospel that is true—
      Christ is not risen!

Is He not risen, and shall we not rise?
    Oh, we unwise!
What did we dream, what wake we to discover?
Ye hills, fall on us, and ye mountains, cover!
    In darkness and great gloom
Come ere we thought it is *our* day of doom;
From the cursed world, which is one tomb,
      Christ is not risen!

Eat, drink and play, and think that this is bliss:
There is no heaven but this;
   There is no hell,
Save earth, which serves the purpose doubly well,
    Seeing it visits still

With equalest apportionment of ill
Both good and bad alike, and brings to one same dust
    The unjust and the just
    With Christ, who is not risen.

Eat, drink and die, for we are souls bereaved:
  Of all the creatures under heaven's wide cope
  We are most hopeless, who had once most hope,
And most beliefless, that had most believed.
    Ashes to ashes, dust to dust;
    As of the unjust, also of the just—
    Yea, of that Just One too!
    It is the one sad Gospel that is true—
      Christ is not risen!

    Weep not beside the tomb,
    Ye women, unto whom
He was great solace while ye tended Him;
    Ye who with napkin o'er the head
And folds of linen round each wounded limb
    Laid out the Sacred Dead;
And thou that bar'st Him in thy wondering womb;
Yet, Daughters of Jerusalem, depart,
Bind up as best ye may your own sad bleeding heart:

Go to your homes, your living children tend,
    Your earthly spouses love;
    Set your affections *not* on things above,
Which moth and rust corrupt, which quickliest come
    to end:
Or pray, if pray ye must, and pray, if pray ye can,
For death; since dead is He whom ye deemed more
      than man,

Who is not risen: no—
But lies and molders low—
   Who is not risen!

   Ye men of Galilee!
Why stand ye looking up to heaven, where Him ye
      never may see,
Neither ascending hence, nor returning hither again?
   Ye ignorant and idle fishermen!
Hence to your huts, and boats, and inland native shore,
   And catch not men, but fish;
   Whatever things ye might wish,
Him neither here nor there ye ever shall meet with
     more.
   Ye poor deluded youths, go home,
   Mend the old nets ye left to roam,
   Tie the split oar, patch the torn sail;
   It was indeed an "idle tale"—
     He was not risen!
And, oh, good men of ages yet to be,
Who shall believe *because* ye did not see—

   Oh, be ye warned, be wise!
   Nor more with pleading eyes,
   And sobs of strong desire,
   Unto the empty vacant void aspire,
Seeking another and impossible birth
That is not of your own, and only mother earth.
But if there is no other life for you,
Sit down and be content, since this must even do;
     He is not risen!
   One look, and then depart,
   Ye humble and ye holy men of heart;
And ye! ye ministers and stewards of a Word

Which ye would preach, because another heard—
 Ye worshippers of that ye do not know,
 Take these things hence and go:
  He is not risen!

 Here, on our Easter Day
We rise, we come, and lo! we find Him not,
Gardener nor other, on the sacred spot:
Where they have laid Him there is none to say;
No sound, nor in, nor out—no word
Of where to seek the dead or meet the living Lord.
There is no glistering of an angel's wings,
There is no voice of heavenly clear behest:
Let us go hence, and think upon these things
 In silence, which is best,
 Is He not risen? No—
 But lies and molders low?
  Christ is not risen?

EASTER DAY

II

So in the sinful streets, abstracted and alone,
 I with my secret self held communing of mine own.
 So in the southern city spake the tongue
Of one that somewhat overwildly sung,
But in a later hour I sat and heard
Another voice that spake—another graver word.
Weep not, it bade, whatever hath been said,
Though He be dead, He is not dead.
 In the true creed
 He is yet risen indeed;
  Christ is yet risen.

ARTHUR HUGH CLOUGH

Weep not beside His Tomb,
Ye women unto whom
He was great comfort and yet greater grief;
Nor ye, ye faithful few that wont with Him to roam,
Seek sadly what for Him ye left, go hopeless to your
    home;
Nor ye despair, ye sharers yet to be of their belief;
    Though He be dead, He is not dead,
    Nor gone, though fled,
    Not lost, though vanishèd;
    Though He return not, though
    He lies and molders low;
    In the true creed
    He is yet risen indeed;
        Christ is yet risen.

Sit if ye will, sit down upon the ground,
Yet not to weep and wail, but calmly look around.
    Whatever befell,
    Earth is not hell:
Now, too, as when it first began,
Life is yet life, and man is man.
For all that breathe beneath the heaven's high cope,
Joy with grief mixes, with despondence hope.
Hope conquers cowardice, joy grief;
Or at least, faith unbelief.
    Though dead, not dead;
    Not gone, though fled;
    Not lost, though vanished,
    In the great gospel and true creed,
    He is yet risen indeed;
        Christ is yet risen.

CHARLES KINGSLEY

ENGLAND, 1819-1875

KINGSLEY was one of the few high impassioned souls in
the English Church. He, with the great Frederick
Maurice, led the Christian Socialist movement in England.
His dramatic songs and poems give hints of Kingsley's
keen sympathy with the tragedy in the lives of the work-
folk. He stood with Carlyle and Ruskin for a new social
order based on justice and humanity.

The Three Fishers

THREE fishers went sailing away to the West,
   Away to the West as the sun went down:
Each thought on the woman who loved him the best,
   And the children stood watching them out of the
      town;
For men must work, and women must weep,
And there's little to earn, and many to keep,
   Though the harbor bar be moaning.

Three wives sat up in the lighthouse tower
   And they trimmed the lamps as the sun went down;
They looked at the squall, and they looked at the shower,
   And the night-rack came rolling up ragged and
      brown.
But men must work, and women must weep,
Though storms be sudden, and waters deep,
   And the harbor bar be moaning.

Three corpses lay out on the shining sands
  In the morning gleam as the tide went down,
And the women are weeping and wringing their hands
  For those who will never come home to the town;
For men must work, and women must weep,
And the sooner it's over, the sooner to sleep;
  And good-by to the bar and its moaning.

The Sands of Dee

O MARY, go and call the cattle home,
    And call the cattle home,
  And call the cattle home,
  Across the sands of Dee."
The western wind was wild and dark with foam,
  And all alone went she.

The western tide crept up along the sand,
    And o'er and o'er the sand,
  And round and round the sand,
  As far as eye could see.
The rolling mist came down and hid the land,
  And never home came she.

"Oh, is it weed, or fish, or floating hair—
    A tress of golden hair,
  A drownèd maiden's hair,
  Above the nets at sea?"
Was never salmon yet that shone so fair
  Among the stakes of Dee.

They rowed her in across the rolling foam,
    The cruel crawling foam,
    The cruel hungry foam,
    To her grave beside the sea.
But still the boatmen hear her call the cattle home,
    Across the sands of Dee.

A Farewell

MY fairest child, I have no song to give you:
    No lark could pipe to skies so dull and gray;
Yet, ere we part, one lesson I can leave you
    For every day.

Be good, sweet maid, and let who will be clever;
    Do noble things, not dream them all day long;
And so make life, death, and that vast forever
    One grand, sweet song.

From "The Day of the Lord"

THE Day of the Lord is at hand, at hand:
    Its storms roll up the sky:
A nation sleeps starving on heaps of gold,
    All dreamers toss and sigh.
The night is darkest before the dawn—
When the pain is sorest the child is born,
    And the Day of the Lord is at hand.

Gather you, gather you, hounds of hell—
Famine and Plague and War;
Idleness, Bigotry, Cant and Misrule,
    Gather and fall in the snare.
Hirlings and Mammonites, Pedants and Knaves,
Crawl to the battle-field—sneak to your graves,
    In the Day of the Lord at hand!

On the Death of a Certain Journal

The "Christian Socialist", started by the Council of Associates for promotion of Industrial Co-operation as the necessary form of Applied Christianity.

SO die, thou child of stormy dawn,
    Thou winter flower, forlorn of nurse;
Chilled early by the bigot's curse,
The pedant's frown, the worldling's yawn.

Fair death, to fall in teeming June,
When every seed which drops to earth
Takes root, and wins a second birth
From steaming shower and gleaming moon.

Fall warm, fall fast, thou mellow rain;
Thou rain of God, make fat the land,
That roots which parch in burning sand
May bud to flower and fruit again,

To grace, perchance, a fairer morn
In mightier lands beyond the sea,
While honor falls to such as we
From hearts of heroes yet unborn,

Who in the light of fuller day,
Of purer science, holier laws,
Bless us, faint heralds of their cause,
Dim beacons of their glorious way.

Failure? While tide-floods rise and boil
Round cape and isle, in port and cove,
Resistless, star-led from above:
What though our tiny wave recoil?

People's Song, 1849

WEEP, weep, weep and weep,
 For pauper, dolt and slave!
Hark from wasted moor and fen,
Feverous alley, workhouse den,
Swells the wail of Saxon men—
Work! or the grave!

Down, down, down and down
With idler, knave and tyrant!
Why for sluggards cark and moil?
He that will not live by toil
Has no right on English soil!
God's word our warrant!

Up, up, up and up!
Face your game and play it.
The night is past, behold the sun—
The idols fall, the lie is done—
The Judge is set, the doom begun!
Who shall stay it?

CHARLES KINGSLEY

A Rough Rhyme on a Rough Matter
THE ENGLISH GAME LAWS

*Here is a terrific cry for justice, an appeal from tyranny to
God. It sounds as if it were torn out of Kingsley's heart.
It is one of the mighty protests made by the poets against
the long plunder of the People by the Few. Eternal honor
to the great English churchman for this thunderbolt from
heaven.*

THE merry brown hares came leaping
  Over the crest of the hill,
Where the clover and corn lay sleeping,
  Under the moonlight still.

Leaping late and early,
  Till under their bite and their tread,
The swedes and the wheat and the barley
  Lay cankered and trampled and dead.

A poacher's widow sat sighing
  On the side of the white chalk bank,
Where, under the gloomy fir-woods,
  One spot in the lea throve rank.

She watched a long tuft of clover,
  Where rabbit or hare never ran;
For its black sour haulm covered over
  The blood of a murdered man.

She thought of the dark plantation,
  And the hares, and her husband's blood;
And the voice of her indignation
  Rose up to the throne of God:

CHARLES KINGSLEY

"I am long past wailing and whining,
  I have wept too much in my life:
I've had twenty years of pining
  As an English laborer's wife.

"A laborer in Christian England,
  Where they cant of a Saviour's name;
And yet waste men's lives, like the vermin's,
  For a few more brace of game.

"There's blood on your new foreign shrubs, squire,
  There's blood on your pointer's feet;
There's blood on the game you sell, squire,
  And there's blood on the game you eat.

"You have sold the laboring man, squire,
  Both body and soul to shame,
To pay for your seat in the House, squire,
  And to pay for the feed of your game.

"You made him a poacher yourself, squire,
  When you'd give neither work nor meat;
And your barley-fed hares robbed the garden
  At our starving children's feet;

"When, packed in one reeking chamber,
  Man, maid, mother and little ones lay;
While the rain pattered in on the rotten bride-bed,
  And the walls let in the day;

"When we lay in the burning fever,
  On the mud of the cold clay floor,
Till you parted us all for three months, squire,
  At the cursèd workhouse door.

CHARLES KINGSLEY

"We quarreled like brutes, and who wonders?
  What self-respect could we keep—
Worse housed than your hacks and your pointers,
  Worse fed than your hogs and your sheep?

"Our daughters, with base-born babies,
  Have wandered away in their shame:
If your misses had slept, squire, where they did,
  Your misses might do the same.

"Can your lady patch hearts that are breaking,
  With handfuls of coals and rice,
Or by dealing out flannel and sheeting
  A little below cost price?

"You may tire of the jail and the workhouse,
  And take to allotments and schools;
But you've run up a debt that will never
  Be repaid us by penny-club rules.

"In the season of shame and sadness,
  In the dark and dreary day,
When scrofula, gout and madness
  Are eating your race away;

"When to kennels and liveried varlets
  You have cast your daughters' bread,
And, worn out with liquor and harlots,
  Your heir at your feet lies dead;

"When your youngest, the mealy-mouthed rector,
  Lets your soul rot asleep to the grave,
You will find in your God the protector
  Of the freeman you fancied your slave."

She looked at the tuft of clover,
  And wept till her heart grew light;
And at last, when her passion was over,
  Went wandering into the night.

But the merry brown hares came leaping
  Over the uplands still,
Where the clover and corn lay sleeping
  On the side of the white chalk hill.

GEORGE ELIOT (MARIAN EVANS CROSS)
ENGLAND, 1819-1880

GEORGE ELIOT, though possessed of great intellect and
sensibility, is not, in respect to metrical expression, a
poet. That wealth of thought which atones for all her
deficiencies in prose does not seem to be at her command in
poetry. *The Spanish Gypsy* reads like a second-rate pro-
duction of the Byronic school. *The Legend of Jubal* and
How Lisa Loved the King suffer by comparison, for instance, with the narrative poems of William Morris and
Longfellow. The following poem in blank verse, setting
forth her conception of the "religion of humanity" is worth
all the rest of her poetry, for, as Stedman says, "it is the
outburst of an exalted soul foregoing personal immortality and compensated by a vision of the growth and
happiness of the human race."

GEORGE ELIOT

O May I Join the Choir Invisible!

O MAY I join the choir invisible
  Of those immortal dead who live again
In minds made better by their presence: live
In pulses stirred to generosity,
In deeds of daring rectitude, in scorn
Of miserable aims that end with self,
In thoughts sublime that pierce the night like stars,
And with their mild persistence urge man's search
To vaster issues.
          So to live is Heaven:
To make undying music in the world,
Breathing as beauteous order that controls
With growing sway the growing life of man.
So we inherit that sweet purity
For which we struggled, failed, and agonized
With widening retrospect that bred despair.
Rebellious flesh that would not be subdued,
A vicious parent shaming still its child
Poor anxious penitence, is quick dissolved;
Its discords, quenched by meeting harmonies,
Die in the large and charitable air.
And all our rarer, better, truer self,
That sobbed religiously in yearning song,
That watched to ease the burthen of the world,
Laboriously tracing what must be,
And what may yet be better—saw within
A worthier image for the sanctuary,
And shaped it forth before the multitude
Divinely human, raising worship so
To higher reverence more mixed with love—
That better self shall live till human Time

Shall fold its eyelids, and the human sky
Be gathered like a scroll within the tomb,
Unread forever.
　　　　　This is life to come,
Which martyred men have made more glorious
For us who strive to follow. May I reach
That purest heaven, be to other souls
The cup of strength in some great agony,
Enkindle generous ardor, feed pure love,
Beget the smiles that have no cruelty—
Be the sweet presence of a good diffused,
And in diffusion ever more intense.
So shall I join the choir invisible
Whose music is the gladness of the world.

JEAN INGELOW
ENGLAND, 1820-1897

From "The High Tide on the Coast of Lincolnshire, 1571"

I

THE old mayor climbed the belfry tower,
　　The ringers ran by two, by three:
"Pull, if ye never pulled before!
　　Good ringers, pull your best!" quoth he.
"Play uppe, play uppe, O Boston bells!
Play all your changes, all your swells—
　　Play uppe 'The Brides of Enderby!'"

JEAN INGELOW

II

I sat and spun within the doore;
  My thread brake off, I raised myne eyes;
The level sun, like ruddy ore,
  Lay sinking in the barren skies;
And dark against day's golden death
She moved where Lindis wandereth—
My sonne's faire wife, Elizabeth.

III

"Cusha! Cusha! Cusha!" calling
Ere the early dews were falling,
Farre away I heard her song.
"Cusha! Cusha!" all along
Where the reedy Lindis floweth,
      Floweth, floweth:
From the meads where melick groweth,
Faintly came her milking-song.

IV

"Cusha! Cusha! Cusha!" calling,
"For the dews will soone be falling;
Leave your meadow grasses mellow,
      Mellow, mellow;
Quit your cowslips, cowslips yellow:
Come uppe, Whitefoot; come uppe, Lightfoot,
Quit the stalks of parsley hollow,
      Hollow, hollow:
Come uppe, Jetty, rise and follow—
From the clovers lift your head;
Come uppe, Whitefoot; come uppe, Lightfoot;

Come uppe, Jetty, rise and follow,
Jetty, to the milking shed."

V

Alle fresh the level pasture lay,
   And not a shadowe mote be seene,
Save where, full fyve good miles away,
   The steeple towered from out the greene;
And lo! the great bell farre and wide
Was heard in all the country-side,
That Saturday at eventide.

VI

I looked without, and lo! my sonne
   Came riding downe with might and main:
He raised a shout as he drew on,
   Till all the welkin rang again—
"Elizabeth! Elizabeth!"
(A sweeter woman ne'er drew breath
Than my sonne's wife, Elizabeth.)

VII

"The olde sea-wall (he cried) is downe:
   The rising tide comes on apace,
And boats adrift in yonder towne
   Go sailing uppe the market-place."
He shook as one that looks on death:
"God save you, mother!" straight he saith;
"Where is my wife, Elizabeth?"

VIII

"Good sonne, where Lindis winds away,
   With her two bairns I marked her long;
And ere yon bells beganne to play,
   Afar I heard her milking-song."
He looked across the grassy lea,
To right, to left—"Ho, Enderby!"
They rang "The Brides of Enderby!"

IX

With that he cried and beat his breast;
   For lo! along the river's bed
A mighty eygre [1] reared his crest,
   And uppe the Lindis raging sped.
It swept with thunderous noises loud—
Shaped like a curling snow-white cloud,
Or like a demon in a shroud.

X

So farre, so fast the eygre drave,
   The heart had hardly time to beat
Before a shallow, seething wave
   Sobbed in the grasses at our feet:
The feet had hardly time to flee
Before it brake against the knee,
And all the world was in the sea.

[1] *Eygre* (ā'-gur), an immense tidal wave.

XI

Upon the roofe we sate that night,
  The noise of bells went sweeping by;
I marked the lofty beacon-light
  Stream from the church-tower, red and high—
A lurid mark and dread to see;
And awesome bells they were to me,
That in the dark rang "Enderby."

XII

They rang the sailor lads to guide
  From roofe to roofe who fearless rowed;
And I—my sonne was at my side,
  And yet the ruddy beacon glowed;
And yet he moaned beneath his breath,
"O, come in life, or come in death!
O, lost! my love, Elizabeth!"

XIII

And didst thou visit him no more?
  Thou didst, thou didst, my daughter deare;
The waters laid thee at his doore,
  Ere yet the early dawn was clear.
Thy pretty bairns in fast embrace,
The lifted sun shone on thy face,
Downe drifted to thy dwelling-place.

XIV

That flow strewed wrecks about the grass,
   That ebbe swept out the flocks to sea—
A fatal ebbe and flow, alas!
   To many more than myne and me:
But each will mourn his own (she saith)
And sweeter woman ne'er drew breath
Than my sonne's wife, Elizabeth.

XV

I shall never hear her more
By the reedy Lindis shore,
"Cusha! Cusha! Cusha!" calling,
Ere the early dews be falling
I shall never hear her song,
"Cusha! Cusha!" all along
Where the sunny Lindis floweth,
     Goeth, floweth,
From the meads where melick groweth,
Where the water, winding down,
Onward floweth to the town.

XVI

I shall never see her more
Where the reeds and rushes quiver,
     Shiver, quiver:
Stand beside the sobbing river,
Sobbing, throbbing, in its falling
To the sandy, lonesome shore.

FREDERICK LOCKER-LAMPSON
ENGLAND, 1821-1895

My Love Is Always Near

MY only love is always near:
  In country or in town
I see her twinkling feet, I hear
  The whisper of her gown.

She foots it ever fair and young:
  Her locks are tied in haste,
And one is over her shoulder flung,
  And hangs below her waist.

She ran before me in the meads;
  And down this world-worn track
She leads me on; but while she leads
  She never gazes back.

And yet her voice is in my dreams,
  To witch me more and more;
That wooing voice! Ah me, it seems
  Less near me than of yore.

Lightly I sped when hope was high,
  And youth beguiled the chase:
I follow, follow still; but I
  Shall never see her face.

MATTHEW ARNOLD
ENGLAND, 1822—1888

LIKE Dryden and Coleridge, Matthew Arnold gained high distinction both as poet and as critic. In his verse we seldom or never detect that "first fine careless rapture"; yet his taste is so cultivated and his mind so clear that, as Edmund Clarence Stedman observes, "he has almost falsified the adage that a poet is born, not made." He is, says Swinburne, the "surest-footed" of modern English poets, the chief qualities of his verse being clearness, simplicity, strong directness, noble and musical rhythm, and a certain intense calm. His shorter poems, as here selected, show Arnold at his austere best.

A note of sadness creeps into Arnold's best poetry. We need not look in him for the cheap discouraging optimism of the poets' corner of the newspaper. He knows of

> "The salt, unplumbed, estranging sea"

that separates us all in our mortal adventure. He ever hears the grating

> "Of pebbles which the waves draw back, and fling
>   At their return, up the high strand,
>   Begin and cease, and then again begin,
>   With tremulous cadence slow, and bring
>   The eternal note of sadness in."

It is the old sadness known to all the lofty and lonely ones:

> "Sophocles long ago
>   Heard it on the Ægean, and it brought
>   Into his mind the turbid ebb and flow
>   Of human misery."

2067

Although he recommends courage and a brave battle, still he knows where we are—

> "For we are here as on a darkling plain,
>   Swept by confused alarms of struggle and flight,
>   Where ignorant armies clash by night."

Always he finds himself

> "Wandering between two worlds—one dead,
>   The other powerless to be born."

And yet

> "The stars come out and the night wind
>   Brings up the stream
>   Murmurs and secrets of the infinite sea."

Moreover,

> "Is it so small a thing
> To have enjoyed the sun;
> To have lived light in the spring;
> To have loved, to have thought, to have done;
> To have advanced true friends, and beat down baffling
>   foes? . . .
> I say, fear not! Life still
> Leaves human effort scope."

Arnold was one of the intellectual giants of the nine-teenth century, and his many prose writings constitute a wholesome body of thought. Upon the basis of his liberal scholarship he erected a creed of life. I quote Gilbert Chesterton's summary of Arnold the thinker:

"Against Mill's 'liberty' and Carlyle's 'strength' and Ruskin's 'nature', Arnold set up a new presence and entity which he called 'culture', the disinterested play of the mind through the sifting of the best books and authorities. Though a little dandified in phrase, he was undoubtedly serious and public-spirited in intention. He sometimes talked of culture almost as if it were a man, or at least a church (for a church has a sort of personality): some suspect that culture was a man, whose name was Matthew Arnold. But Arnold was not only right but highly valuable. . . . He was a sort of Heaven-sent courier. His frontal attack on the vulgar and sullen optimism of Victorian utility may be summed up in the admirable sentence, in which he asked the English what was the use of a train taking them quickly from Islington to Camberwell, if it only took them 'from a dismal and illiberal life in Islington to a dismal and illiberal life in Camberwell?' "

In poetry Arnold was chiefly under the influence of Wordsworth. But he never has the Wordsworthian slips into the prosaic quagmire. He never (like Wordsworth) mixes masses of enormous dullness with the precious substance fallen from the stars. And he does not follow Wordsworth in apologizing for the nature of things: so we find him facing the facts of our existence, and calmly beholding in them the presence of a pathetic fate. But we must meet our doom with a quiet resignation; so he becomes the outstanding poet of modern stoicism.

Arnold threw into modern poetry a remarkable infusion of Hellenic thought and feeling; but he moves ever in a mist of sadness, while the Greek was ever in the light of joy.

To Marguerite

The concluding line of this poem is most impressive. "Without any false emphasis or prolix dwelling on the matter," to quote Richard Holt Hutton, "it shadows out to you the plunging deep-sea lead and the eerie cry of 'no soundings': it recalls that saltness of the sea which takes from water every refreshing association, every quality that helps to slake thirst or supply sap, and then it concentrates all these dividing attributes, which srike a sort of lonely terror into the soul, into the one word 'estrang-

ing.' It is a line full of intensity, simplicity and grandeur —a line to possess and haunt the imagination. And the same exceptional force of expression comes out not unfrequently under the shadow of similar emotion."

YES; in the sea of life enisled,
  With echoing straits between us thrown,
Dotting the shoreless watery wild,
  We mortal millions live *alone*.
The islands feel the enclasping flow,
And then their endless bounds they know.

But when the moon their hollows lights,
  And they are swept by balms of spring,
And in their glens, on starry nights,
  The nightingales divinely sing;
And lovely notes, from shore to shore,
Across the sounds and channels pour;

Oh, then a longing like despair
  Is to their farthest caverns sent!
For surely once, they feel, we were
  Parts of a single continent.
Now round us spreads the watery plain—
Oh, might our marges meet again!

Who ordered that their longing's fire
  Should be, as soon as kindled, cooled?
Who renders vain their deep desire?
  A God, a God their severance ruled;
And bade betwixt their shores to be
The unplumbed, salt, estranging sea.

MATTHEW ARNOLD

Requiescat

STREW on her roses, roses,
    And never a spray of yew.
In quiet she reposes:
    Ah! would that I did too.

Her mirth the world required:
    She bathed it in smiles of glee.
But her heart was tired, tired,
    And now they let her be.

Her life was turning, turning,
    In mazes of heat and sound.
But for peace her soul was yearning,
    And now peace laps her round.

Her cabined, ample Spirit,
    It fluttered and failed for breath.
To-night it doth inherit
    The vasty hall of Death.

Philomela

HARK! ah, the nightingale!
    The tawny-throated!
Hark! from that moonlit cedar what a burst!
What triumph! hark—what pain!

O wanderer from a Grecian shore,
Still, after many years, in distant lands,
Still nourishing in thy bewildered brain
That wild, unquenched, deep-sunken, old-world pain—

Say, will it never heal?
And can this fragrant lawn
With its cool trees, and night,
And the sweet, tranquil Thames,
And moonshine, and the dew,
To thy racked heart and brain
Afford no balm?

Dost thou to-night behold
Here, through the moonlight on this English grass,
The unfriendly palace in the Thracian wild?
Dost thou again peruse
With hot cheeks and seared eyes
The too clear web, and thy dumb Sister's shame?
Dost thou once more assay
Thy flight, and feel come over thee,
Poor Fugitive, the feathery change
Once more, and once more seem to make resound
With love and hate, triumph and agony,
Lone Daulis, and the high Cephissian vale?
Listen, Eugenia—
How thick the bursts came crowding through the leaves!
Again—thou hearest!
Eternal Passion!
Eternal Pain!

Shakespeare

OTHERS abide our question. Thou art free.
We ask and ask: thou smilest and art still,
Out-topping knowledge. For the loftiest hill
That to the stars uncrowns his majesty,
Planting his steadfast footsteps in the sea,
Making the heaven of heavens his dwelling-place,
Spares but the cloudy border of his base
To the foiled searching of mortality;

And thou, who didst the stars and sunbeams know,
Self-schooled, self-scanned, self-honored, self-secure,
Didst walk on earth unguessed at. Better so!
All pains the immortal spirit must endure,
  All weakness that impairs, all griefs that bow,
  Find their sole voice in that victorious brow.

From "Empedocles on Etna"

THE Gods laugh in their sleeve
    To watch man doubt and fear,
Who knows not what to believe
Since he sees nothing clear,
And dares stamp nothing false where he finds nothing
    sure.

Is this, Pausanias, so?
And can our souls not strive,
  But with the winds must go,
  And hurry where they drive?
Is fate indeed so strong, man's strength indeed so poor?

* * * * *

These hundred doctors try
To preach thee to their school.
"We have the truth!" they cry;
  And yet their oracle,
Trumpet it as they will, is but the same as thine.

Once read thy own breast right,
And thou hast done with fears:
Man gets no other light,
  Search he a thousand years.
Sink in thyself! there ask what ails thee, at that shrine!

What makes thee struggle and rave?
Why are men ill at ease?
'Tis that the lot they have
Fails their own will to please:
For man would make no murmuring, were his will
    obeyed.

And why is it, that still
Man with his lot thus fights?
'Tis that he makes this *will*
The measure of his *rights,*
And believes Nature outraged if his will's gainsaid.

Couldst thou, Pausanias, learn
How deep a fault is this;
Couldst thou but once discern
Thou has no *right* to bliss,
No title from the Gods to welfare and repose;

Then thou wouldst look less mazed
Whene'er of bliss debarred,
Nor think the Gods were crazed
When thy own lot went hard.
But we are all the same—the fools of our own woes!

For, from the first faint morn
Of life, the thirst for bliss
Deep in man's heart is born;
And, skeptic as he is,
He fails not to judge clear if this be quenched or no.

Nor is the thirst to blame.
Man errs not that he deems
His welfare his true aim,

He errs because he dreams
The world does but exist that welfare to bestow.

We mortals are no kings
For each of whom to sway
A new-made world up-springs,
Meant merely for his play;
No, we are strangers here; the world is from of old.

In vain our pent wills fret,
And would the world subdue.
Limits we did not set
Condition all we do;
Born into life we are, and life must be our mold.

Born into life!—man grows
Forth from his parents' stem,
And blends their bloods, as those
Of theirs are blent in them;
So each new man strikes root into a far fore-time.

Born into life!—we bring
A bias with us here,
And, when here, each new thing
Affects us we come near;
To tunes we did not call our being must keep chime.

Riches we wish to get,
Yet remain spendthrifts still;
We would have health, and yet
Still use our bodies ill;
Bafflers of our own prayers, from youth to life's last
    scenes.

We would have inward peace,
Yet will not look within;
We would have misery cease,
Yet will not cease from sin;
We want all pleasant ends, but will use no harsh means;

We do not what we ought,
What we ought not, we do,
And lean upon the thought
That chance will bring us through;
But our own acts, for good or ill, are mightier powers.

Yet, even when man forsakes
All sin—is just, is pure,
Abandons all which makes
His welfare insecure—
Other existences there are, that clash with ours.

Like us, the lightning-fires
Love to have scope and play;
The stream, like us, desires
An unimpeded way:
Like us, the Libyan wind delights to roam at large.

Streams will not curb their pride
The just man not to entomb,
Nor lightnings go aside
To give his virtues room;
Nor is that wind less rough which blows a good man's
    barge.

Nature, with equal mind,
Sees all her sons at play;
Sees man control the wind,

The wind sweep man away;
Allows the proudly-riding and the foundering bark.

And, lastly, though of ours
No weakness spoil our lot,
Though the non-human powers
Of Nature harm us not,
The ill deeds of other men make often *our* life dark.

* * * * *

So, loath to suffer mute,
We, peopling the void air,
Make Gods to whom to impute
The ills we ought to bear;
With God and Fate to rail at, suffering easily.

Yet grant—as sense long missed
Things that are now perceived,
And much may still exist
Which is not yet believed—
Grant that the world were full of Gods we cannot see;

All things the world which fill
Of but one stuff are spun,
That we who rail are still,
With what we rail at, one;
One with the o'erlabored Power that through the
  breadth and length

Of earth, and air, and sea,
In men, and plants, and stones,
Hath toil perpetually,
And travails, pants and moans;
Fain would do all things well, but sometimes fails in
  strength.

And patiently exact
This universal God
Alike to any act
Proceeds at any nod.
And quietly declaims the cursings of himself.

This is not what man hates,
Yet he can curse but this,
Harsh Gods and hostile Fates
Are dreams! this only *is*,
Is everywhere; sustains the wise, the foolish elf

Not only, in the intent
To attach blame elsewhere,
Do we at will invent
Stern Powers who make their care
To embitter human life, malignant Deities;

But, next, we would reverse
The scheme ourselves have spun,
And what we made to curse
We now would lean upon,
And feign kind Gods who perfect what man vainly tries.

* * * * *

Fools! That in man's brief term
He cannot all things view,
Affords no ground to affirm
That there are Gods who do;
Nor does being weary prove that he has where to rest.

Again—Our youthful blood
Claims rapture as its right;
The world, a rolling flood
Of newness and delight,
Draws in the enamored gazer to its shining breast;

Pleasure, to our hot grasp,
Gives flowers after flowers;
With passionate warmth we clasp
Hand after hand in ours;
Now do we soon perceive how fast our youth is spent.

At once our eyes grow clear!
We see, in blank dismay,
Year posting after year,
Sense after sense decay;
Our shivering heart is mined by secret discontent;

Yet still, in spite of truth,
In spite of hopes entombed,
That longing of our youth
Burns ever unconsumed,
Still hungrier for delight as delights grow more rare.

We pause; we hush our heart,
And thus address the Gods:
"The world hath failed to impart
The joy our youth forebodes,
Failed to fill up the void which in our breast we bear.

"Changeful till now, we still
Looked on to something new;
Let us, with changeless will,
Henceforth look on to you,
To find with you the joy we in vain here require!"

Fools! That so often here
Happiness mocked our prayer,
I think, might make us fear
A like event elsewhere;
Make us, not fly to dreams, but moderate desire.

And yet, for those who know
Themselves, who wisely take
Their way through life, and bow
To what they cannot break,
Why should I say that life need yield but *moderate*
bliss?

Shall we, with temper spoiled,
Health sapped by living ill,
And judgment all embroiled
By sadness and self-will,
Shall *we* judge what for man is not true bliss or is?

Is it so small a thing
To have enjoyed the sun,
To have lived light in the spring,
To have loved, to have thought, to have done;
To have advanced true friends, and beat down baffling
foes—

That we must feign a bliss
Of doubtful future date,
And, while we dream on this,
Lose all our present state,
And relegate to worlds yet distant our repose?

Not much, I know, you prize
What pleasures may be had,
Who look on life with eyes
Estranged, like mine, and sad;
And yet the village-churl feels the truth more than you.

Who's loath to leave this life
Which to him little yields—
His hard-tasked sunburnt wife,

His often-labored fields,
The boors with whom he talked, the country-spots he
  knew.

But thou, because thou hearest
Men scoff at Heaven and Fate,
Because the Gods thou fearest
Fail to make blest thy state,
Tremblest, and wilt not dare to trust the joys there are!

I say: Fear not! Life still
Leaves human effort scope.
But, since life teems with ill,
Nurse no extravagant hope;
Because thou must not dream, thou needest not then
  despair!

Callicles' Song

FROM "EMPEDOCLES ON ETNA"

THROUGH the black, rushing smoke-
    bursts,
Thick breaks the red flame;
All Etna heaves fiercely
Her forest-clothed frame.

Not here, O Apollo!
Are haunts meet for thee.
But, where Helicon breaks down
In cliff to the sea,

Where the moon-silvered inlets
Send far their light voice
Up the still vale of Thisbe,
O speed, and rejoice!

On the sward at the cliff-top
Lie strewn the white flocks,
On the cliff-side the pigeons
Roost deep in the rocks.

In the moonlight the shepherds,
Soft lulled by the rills,
Lie wrapped in their blankets
Asleep on the hills.

What forms are these coming
So white through the gloom?
What garments out-glistening
The gold-flowered broom?

What sweet-breathing presence
Out-perfumes the thyme?
What voices enrapture
The night's balmy prime?

'Tis Apollo comes leading
His choir, the Nine.
The leader is fairest,
But all are divine.

They are lost in the hollows!
They stream up again!
What seeks on this mountain
The glorified train?

They bathe on this mountain,
In the spring by their road;
Then on to Olympus,
Their endless abode.

Whose praise do they mention?
Of what is it told?
What will be for ever;
What was from of old.

First hymn they the Father
Of all things; and then,
The rest of immortals,
The action of men;

The day in his hotness,
The strife with the palm;
The night in her silence,
The stars in their calm.

Austerity of Poetry

THAT son of Italy who tried to blow,
   Ere Dante came, the trump of sacred song,
In his light youth amid a festal throng
Sate with his bride to see a public show.
Fair was the bride, and on her front did glow
   Youth like a star; and what to youth belong—
   Gay raiment, sparkling gauds, elation strong.
A prop gave way! crash fell a platform! Lo,

Mid struggling sufferers, hurt to death, she lay!
   Shuddering, they drew her garments off—and found
   A robe of sackcloth next the smooth, white skin.
Such, poets, is your bride, the Muse! young, gay,
   Radiant, adorned outside; a hidden ground
   Of thought and of austerity within.

MATTHEW ARNOLD

Dover Beach

THE sea is calm to-night.
   The tide is full, the moon lies fair
Upon the straits; on the French coast the light
Gleams and is gone; the cliffs of England stand,
Glimmering and vast, out in the tranquil bay.
Come to the window, sweet is the night-air!
Only, from the long line of spray
Where the sea meets the moon-blanched land,
Listen! you hear the grating roar
Of pebbles which the waves draw back, and fling,
At their return, up the high strand,
Begin, and cease, and then again begin,
With tremulous cadence slow, and bring
The eternal note of sadness in.

Sophocles long ago
Heard it on the Ægæan, and it brought
Into his mind the turbid ebb and flow
Of human misery; we
Find also in the sound a thought,
Hearing it by this distant northern sea.

The Sea of Faith
Was once, too, at the full, and round earth's shore
Lay like the folds of a bright girdle furled.
But now I only hear
Its melancholy, long, withdrawing roar,
Retreating, to the breath
Of the night-wind, down the vast edges drear
And naked shingles of the world.

Ah, Love, let us be true
To one another! for the world, which seems
To lie before us like a land of dreams,

So various, so beautiful, so new,
Hath really neither joy, nor love, nor light,
Nor certitude, nor peace, nor help for pain;
And we are here as on a darkling plain
Swept with confused alarms of struggle and flight,
Where ignorant armies clash by night.

Memorial Verses
(APRIL, 1850)

*In this poem are brought out the salient points of three
poets who had recently died—Byron, Goethe and Wordsworth. The characteristics of Byron's and Goethe's genius
are portrayed with an insight and comprehensiveness un-
surpassed in Arnold's best prose criticism. He praises
Wordsworth for the power of exciting free, happy emotion,
and for his recognition in nature of a mysterious kinship
with man, investing her beauty and grandeur with spiritual
significance.*

GOETHE in Weimar sleeps; and Greece,
Long since, saw Byron's struggle cease.
But one such death remained to come:
The last poetic voice is dumb—
We stand to-day by Wordsworth's tomb.

When Byron's eyes were shut in death,
We bowed our head, and held our breath.
He taught us little, but our soul
Had *felt* him like the thunder's roll.
With shivering heart the strife we saw
Of passion with eternal law;
And yet with reverential awe
We watched the fount of fiery life
Which served for that Titanic strife.

When Goethe's death was told, we said:
Sunk, then, is Europe's sagest head.
Physician of the iron age,
Goethe has done his pilgrimage.
He took the suffering human race,
He read each wound, each weakness clear;
And struck his finger on the place,
And said: *Thou ailest here, and here!*
He looked on Europe's dying hour
Of fitful dream and feverish power;
His eye plunged down the weltering strife,
The turmoil of expiring life:
He said: *The end is everywhere,*
Art still has truth, take refuge there!
And he was happy, if to know
Causes of things, and far below
His feet to see the lurid flow
Of terror, and insane distress,
And headlong fate, be happiness.

And Wordsworth! Ah, pale ghosts, rejoice!
For never has such soothing voice
Been to your shadowy world conveyed,
Since erst, at morn, some wandering shade
Heard the clear song of Orpheus come
Through Hades and the mournful gloom.
Wordsworth has gone from us; and ye,
Ah, may ye feel his voice as we!
He too upon a wintry clime
Had fallen—on this iron time
Of doubts, disputes, distractions, fears.
He found us when the age had bound
Our souls in its benumbing round;
He spoke, and loosed our heart in tears.

MATTHEW ARNOLD

He laid us as we lay at birth
On the cool flowery lap of earth:
Smiles broke from us, and we had ease;
The hills were round us, and the breeze
Went o'er the sunlit fields again;
Our foreheads felt the wind and rain.
Our youth returned; for there was shed
On spirits that had long been dead,
Spirits dried up and closely furled,
The freshness of the early world.

Ah! since dark days still bring to light
Man's prudence and man's fiery might,
Time may restore us in his course
Goethe's sage mind and Byron's force;
But where will Europe's latter hour
Again find Wordsworth's healing power?
Others will teach us how to dare,
And against fear our breast to steel:
Others will strengthen us to bear—
But who, ah! who will make us feel?
The cloud of mortal destiny,
Others will front it fearlessly;
But who, like him, will put it by?
Keep fresh the grass upon his grave,
O Rotha,[1] with thy living wave!
Sing him thy best! for few or none
Hear thy voice right, now he is gone.

[1] Rotha, the stream by which Wordsworth is buried. See the
first stanza of *Wordsworth's Grave*, by William Watson.

MATTHEW ARNOLD

The Good Shepherd with the Kid

HE saves the sheep, the goats he doth not save.
    So rang Tertullian's sentence, on the side
Of that unpitying Phrygian sect which cried:
"Him can no fount of fresh forgiveness lave,
Who sins, once washed by the baptismal wave."
    So spake the fierce Tertullian. But she sighed,
    The infant Church! of love she felt the tide
Stream on her from her Lord's yet recent grave.

And then she smiled; and in the Catacombs,
    With eye suffused but heart inspired true,
On those walls subterranean, where she hid
Her head 'mid ignominy, death, and tombs,
    She her Good Shepherd's hasty image drew—
And on his shoulders, not a lamb, a kid.

Stanzas from "The Grand Chartreuse"

*The poet climbs, mule-back, into the Alps to an old palace
of the kings of France, now turned into a monastery; and
there he ponders again the difficult and anxious problem
of how to live life—a problem ever near to his heart.*

APPROACH, for what we seek is here!
    Alight, and sparely sup, and wait
For rest in this outbuilding near;
Then cross the sward and reach that gate.
Knock; pass the wicket! Thou art come
To the Carthusians' world-famed home.

MATTHEW ARNOLD

The silent courts, where night and day
Into their stone-carved basins cold
The splashing icy fountains play—
The humid corridors behold!
Where, ghostlike in the deepening night
Cowled forms brush by in gleaming white.

The chapel, where no organ's peal
Invests the stern and naked prayer—
With penitential cries they kneel
And wrestle; rising then, with bare
And white uplifted faces stand,
Passing the Host from hand to hand.

Each takes, and then his visage wan
Is buried in his cowl once more.
The cells!—the suffering Son of Man
Upon the wall—the knee-worn floor—
And where they sleep, that wooden bed,
Which shall their coffin be, when dead!

The garden, overgrown—yet mild,
See, fragrant herbs are flowering there!
Strong children of the Alpine wild
Whose culture is the brethren's care;
Of human tasks their only one,
And cheerful works beneath the sun.

Those halls, too, destined to contain
Each its own pilgrim-host of old,
From England, Germany, or Spain—
All are before me! I behold
The House, the Brotherhood austere!
And what am I, that I am here?

For rigorous teachers seized my youth,
And purged its faith, and trimmed its fire,
Showed me the high, white star of Truth,
There bade me gaze, and there aspire.
Even now their whispers pierce the gloom;
What dost thou in this living tomb?

Forgive me, masters of the mind!
At whose behest I long ago
So much unlearnt, so much resigned—
I come not here to be your foe!
I seek these anchorites, not in ruth,
To curse and to deny your truth;

Not as their friend, or child, I speak!
But as, on some far northern strand,
Thinking of his own Gods, a Greek
In pity and mournful awe might stand
Before some fallen Runic stone—
For both were faiths, and both are gone.

Wandering between two worlds, one dead,
The other powerless to be born,
With nowhere yet to rest my head,
Like these, on earth I wait forlorn.
Their faith, my tears, the world deride—
I come to shed them at their side.

Oh, hide me in your gloom profound,
Ye solemn seats of holy pain!
Take me, cowled forms, and fence me **round**
Till I possess my soul again;
Till free my thoughts before me roll,
Not chafed by hourly false control!

For the world cries your faith is now
But a dead time's exploded dream;
My melancholy, sciolists say,
Is a passed mode, an outworn theme—
As if the world had ever had
A faith, or sciolists been sad!

Ah, if it *be* passed, take away,
At least, the restlessness, the pain:
Be man henceforth no more a prey
To these out-dated stings again!
The nobleness of grief is gone—
Ah, leave us not the fret alone!

But—if you cannot give us ease—
Last of the race of them who grieve
Here leave us to die out with these
Last of the people who believe!
Silent, while years engrave the brow;
Silent—the best are silent now.

Achilles ponders in his tent,
The kings of modern thought are dumb;
Silent they are, though not content,
And wait to see the future come.
They have the grief men had of yore,
But they contend and cry no more.

Our fathers watered with their tears
This sea of time whereon we sail,
Their voices were in all men's ears
We passed within their puissant hail.
Still the same ocean round us raves,
But we stand mute, and watch the waves.

MATTHEW ARNOLD

For what availed it, all the noise
And outcry of the former men?
Say, have their sons achieved more joys,
Say, is life lighter now than then;
The sufferers died, they left their pain—
The pangs which tortured them remain.

What helps it now, that Byron bore,
With haughty scorn which mocked the smart,
Through Europe to the Ætolian shore
The pageant of his bleeding heart?
That thousands counted every groan,
And Europe made his woe her own?

What boots it, Shelley! that the breeze
Carried thy lovely wail away,
Musical through Italian trees
Which fringe thy soft blue Spezzian bay?
Inheritors of thy distress
Have restless hearts one throb the less?

Or are we easier, to have read,
O Obermann! the sad, stern page,
Which tells us how thou hidd'st thy head
From the fierce tempest of thine age
In the lone brakes of Fontainebleau,
Or chalets near the Alpine snow?

Years hence, perhaps, may dawn an age,
More fortunate, alas! than we,
Which without hardness will be sage,
And gay without frivolity.
Sons of the world, oh, speed those years;
But, while we wait, allow our tears!

Allow them! We admire with awe
The exulting thunder of your race:
You give the universe your law,
You triumph over time and space!
Your tide of life, your tireless powers,
We laud them, but they are not ours.

A Summer Night

*Here we come upon "A Summer Night" followed by "The
Buried Life", two poems that rise to the high summit of
Arnold's powers. Nowhere else in modern poetry do we
get so poignant a sense of the doom under which we move,
and of the emptiness of all those prizes for which we battle
and die. These poems are springtides of his spirit, and
they proclaim the noble and tender ideality from which his
lyric cries proceed.*

IN the deserted, moon-blanched street,
  How lonely rings the echo of my feet!
Those windows, which I gaze at, frown,
Silent and white, unopening down,
Repellant as the world—but see,
A break between the housetops shows
The moon! and, lost behind her, fading dim
Into the dewy park obscurity
Down at the far horizon's rim,
Doth a whole tract of heaven disclose!
And to my mind the thought
Is on a sudden brought
Of a past night, and a far different scene.
Headlands stood out into the moonlit deep
As clearly as at noon;
The spring-tide's brimming flow
Heaved dazzlingly between;

Houses, with long white sweep,
Girdled the glistening bay;
Behind, through the soft air,
The blue haze-cradled mountains spread away,
The night was far more fair—
But the same restless pacings to and fro,
And the same vainly throbbing heart was there,
And the same bright, calm moon.

And the calm moonlight seems to say:
Hast thou then still the old unquiet breast,
Which neither deadens into rest,
Nor ever feels the fiery glow
That whirls the spirit from itself away,
But fluctuates to and fro,
Never by passion quite possessed
And never quite benumbed by the world's sway?
And I, I know not if to pray
Still to be what I am, or yield and be
Like all the other men I see.

For most men in a brazen prison live,
Where, in the sun's hot eye,
With heads bent o'er their toil, they languidly
Their lives to some unmeaning taskwork give,
Dreaming of nought beyond their prison wall.
And as, year after year,
Fresh products of their barren labor fall
From their tired hands, and rest
Never yet comes more near,
Gloom settles slowly down over their breast;
And while they try to stem
The waves of mournful thought by which they are
        pressed,

Death in their prison reaches them,
Unfreed, having seen nothing, still unblest.
And the rest, a few,
Escape their prison and depart
On the wide ocean of life anew.
There the freed prisoner, where'er his heart
Listeth, will sail;
Nor doth he know how there prevail,
Despotic on that sea,
Trade-winds which cross it from eternity.

Awhile he holds some false way, undebarred
By thwarting signs, and braves
The freshening wind and blackening waves
And then the tempest strikes him; and between
The lightning-bursts is seen
Only a driving wreck,
And the pale master on his spar-strewn deck
With anguished face and flying hair
Grasping the rudder hard,
Still bent to make some port he knows not where,
Still standing for some false, impossible shore.
And sterner comes the roar
Of sea and wind, and through the deepening gloom
Fainter and fainter wreck and helmsman loom,
And he too disappears, and comes no more.

Is there no life, but these alone?
Madman or slave, must man be one?

Plainness and clearness without shadow of stain!
Clearness divine!
Ye heavens, whose pure dark regions have no sign
Of languor, though so calm, and, though so great,

Are yet untroubled and unpassionate;
Who, though so noble, share in the world's toil,
And, though so tasked, keep free from dust and soil!
I will not say that your mild deeps retain
A tinge, it may be, of their silent pain
Who have longed deeply once, and longed in vain—
But I will rather say that you remain
A world above man's head, to let him see
How boundless might his soul's horizons be,
How vast, yet of what clear transparency!
How it were good to abide there, and breathe free;
How fair a lot to fill
Is left to each man still!

The Buried Life

LIGHT flows our war of mocking words; and yet
    Behold, with tears mine eyes are wet!
I feel a nameless sadness o'er me roll.
Yes, yes, we know that we can jest,
We know, we know, that we can smile!
But there's a something in this breast,
To which thy light words bring no rest,
And thy gay smiles no anodyne;
Give me thy hand, and hush awhile,
And turn those limpid eyes on mine,
And let me read there, Love, thy inmost soul.

    Alas! is even love too weak
To unlock the heart and let it speak?
Are even lovers powerless to reveal
To one another what indeed they feel?
I knew the mass of common men concealed

Their thoughts, for fear that if revealed
They would by other men be met
With blank indifference, or with blame reproved;
I knew they lived and moved
Tricked in disguises, alien to the rest
Of men, and alien to themselves—and yet
The same heart beats in every human breast!
But we, my Love! doth a like spell benumb
Our hearts, our voices? Must we, too, be dumb?
Ah, well for us, if even we,
Even for a moment, can get free
Our heart, and have our lips unchained;
For that which seals them hath been deep ordained!
Fate, which foresaw
How frivolous a baby man would be—
By what distractions he would be possessed,
How he would pour himself in every strife,
And well-nigh change his own identity—
That it might keep from his capricious play
His genuine self, and force him to obey
Even in his own despite his being's law,
Bade through the deep recesses of our breast
The unregarded river of our life
Pursue with indiscernible flow its way;
And that we should not see
The buried stream, and seem to be
Eddying at large in blind uncertainty,
Though driving on with it eternally.

But often, in the world's most crowded streets,
But often, in the din of strife,
There rises an unspeakable desire
After the knowledge of our buried life,
A thirst to spend our fire and restless force
In tracking out our true, original course;

A longing to inquire
Into the mystery of this heart which beats
So wild, so deep in us—to know
Whence our lives come, and where they go.
And many a man in his own breast then delves,
But deep enough, alas! none ever mines.
And we have been on many thousand lines,
And we have shown, on each, spirit and power;
But hardly have we, for one little hour,
Been on our own line, have we been ourselves—
Hardly had skill to utter one of all
The nameless feelings that course throughout our **breast,**
But they course on forever unexpressed.
And long we try in vain to speak and act
Our hidden self, and what we say and do
Is eloquent, is well—but 'tis not true!
And then we will no more be racked
With inward striving, and demand
Of all the thousand nothings of the hour
Their stupefying power,
Ah, yes, and they benumb us at our call!

Yet still, from time to time, vague and forlorn,
From the soul's subterranean depth upborne
As from an infinitely distant land,
Come airs, and floating echoes and convey
A melancholy into all our day.

Only—but this is rare—
When a beloved hand is laid in ours,
When, jaded with the rush and glare
Of the interminable hours,
Our eyes can in another's eyes read clear,
When our world-deafened ear
Is by the tones of a loved voice caressed,—

A bolt is shot back somewhere in our breast,
And a lost pulse of feeling stirs again.
The eye sinks inward, and the heart lies plain,
And what we mean, we say, and what we would, we
    know.

A man becomes aware of his life's flow,
And hears its winding murmur, and he sees
The meadows where it glides, the sun, the breeze.

And there arrives a lull in the hot race
Wherein he doth forever chase
The flying and elusive phantom, rest.
An air of coolness plays upon his face,
And an unwonted calm pervades his breast;
And then he thinks he knows
The hills where his life rose,
And the sea where it goes.

Thyrsis

A Monody

"Thyrsis", which ranks with Milton's "Lycidas", Shelley's "Adonais", and Swinburne's "Ave atque Vale" as one of the four noblest English elegies, was written in commemoration of Arthur Hugh Clough, who died in Florence, Italy, in 1861. He and Arnold were classmates and devoted friends at Rugby and Oxford. Thyrsis is the name of a herdsman in the "Idyls" of Theocritus, also of a shepherd in the "Eclogues" of Virgil. In this monody we have the lament of a loyal soul over one who had shared his own deep intimacy with nature in the dearest of all the quiet places of England to scholarly minds—of a baffled inquirer bereft of the partner of his researches—of a steadfast soldier over the comrade who has fallen by his side in an ever doubtful battle.

HOW changed is here each spot man makes or fills!
  In the two Hinkseys nothing keeps the same;
    The village-street its haunted mansion lacks,
And from the sign is gone Sibylla's name,
    And from the roofs the twisted chimney-stacks—
      Are ye too changed, ye hills?
See, 'tis no foot of unfamiliar men
    To-night from Oxford up your pathway strays!
    Here came I often, often, in old days—
Thyrsis and I; we still had Thyrsis then.

Runs it not here, the track by Childsworth Farm,
    Past the high wood, to where the elm-tree crowns
      The hill behind whose ridge the sunset flames?
The signal-elm, that looks on Ilsley Downs,
    The Vale, the three lone weirs, the youthful
        Thames?—
      This winter-eve is warm,
Humid the air! leafless, yet soft as spring,
    The tender purple spray on copse and briers!
    And that sweet city with her dreaming spires,
She needs not June for beauty's heightening,

Lovely all times she lies, lovely to-night!—
    Only, methinks, some loss of habit's power
      Befalls me wandering through this upland dim.
Once passed I blindfold here, at any hour;
    Now seldom come I, since I came with him.
      That single elm-tree bright
Against the west—I miss it! is it gone?
    We prized it dearly; while it stood, we said,
    Our friend, the Gipsy-Scholar, was not dead;
While the tree lived, he in these fields lived on.

Too rare, too rare, grow now my visits here,
  But once I knew each field, each flower, each stick;
    And with the country-folk acquaintance made
By barn in threshing-time, by new-built rick.
    Here, too, our shepherd-pipes we first assayed.
      Ah me! this many a year
My pipe is lost, my shepherd's holiday!
    Needs must I lose them, needs with heavy heart
    Into the world and wave of men depart;
But Thrysis of his own will went away.

It irked him to be here, he could not rest.
  He loved each simple joy the country yields,
    He loved his mates; but yet he could not keep,
For that a shadow loured on the fields,
    Here with the shepherds and the silly sheep.
      Some life of men unblest
He knew, which made him droop, and filled his head
    He went; his piping took a troubled sound
    Of storms that rage outside our happy ground;
He could not wait their passing, he is dead.

So, some tempestuous morn in early June,
  When the year's primal burst of bloom is o'er,
    Before the roses and the longest day—
When garden-walks and all the grassy floor
    With blossoms red and white of fallen May
      And chestnut-flowers are strewn—
So have I heard the cuckoo's parting cry,
    From the wet field, through the vexed garden-trees,
    Come with the volleying rain and tossing breeze:
The bloom is gone, and with the bloom go I!

Too quick despairer, wherefore wilt thou go?
 Soon will the high Midsummer pomps come on,
  Soon will the musk carnations break and swell,
 Soon shall we have gold-dusted snapdragon,
  Sweet-William with his homely cottage-smell,
   And stocks in fragrant blow;
 Roses that down the alleys shine afar,
  And open, jasmine-muffled lattices,
  And groups under the dreaming garden-trees,
 And the full moon, and the white evening-star.

He hearkens not! light comer, he is flown!
 What matters it? next year he will return,
  And we shall have him in the sweet spring-days,
 With whitening hedges, and uncrumpling fern,
  And blue-bells trembling by the forest-ways,
   And scent of hay new-mown.
 But Thyrsis never more we swains shall see;
  See him come back, and cut a smoother reed,
  And blow a strain the world at last shall heed—
 For Time, not Corydon, hath conquered thee!

Alack, for Corydon no rival now!—
 But when Sicilian shepherds lost a mate,
  Some good survivor with his flute would go,
 Piping a ditty sad for Bion's fate;
  And cross the unpermitted ferry's flow,
   And relax Pluto's brow,
 And make leap up with joy the beauteous head
  Of Proserpine, among whose crowned hair
  Are flowers first opened on Sicilian air,
 And flute his friend, like Orpheus, from the dead.

O easy access to the hearer's grace
  When Dorian shepherds sang to Proserpine!
    For she herself had trod Sicilian fields,
  She knew the Dorian water's gush divine,
    She knew each lily white which Enna yields,
      Each rose with blushing face:
  She loved the Dorian pipe, the Dorian strain.
    But ah, of our poor Thames she never heard!
    Her foot the Cumner cowslips never stirred;
  And we should tease her with our plaint in vain!

Well! wind-dispersed and vain the words will be,
  Yet, Thyrsis, let me give my grief its hour
    In the old haunt, and find our tree-topped hill!
  Who, if not I, for questing here hath power?
    I know the wood which hides the daffodil,
      I know the Fyfield tree,
  I know what white, what purple fritillaries
    The grassy harvest of the river-fields,
    Above by Ensham, down by Sandford, yields,
  And what sedged brooks are Thames's tributaries;

I know these slopes; who knows them if not I?
  But many a dingle on the loved hill-side,
    With thorns once studded, old, white-blossomed
      trees,
  Where thick the cowslips grew, and far descried
    High towered the spikes of purple orchises,
      Hath since our day put by
  The coronals of that forgotten time;
    Down each green bank hath gone the ploughboy's
      team,
    And only in the hidden brookside gleam
  Primroses, orphans of the flowery prime.

Where is the girl, who by the boatman's door,
　　Above the locks, above the boating throng,
　　　　Unmoored our skiff when through the Wytham
　　　　　　flats,
　　Red loosestrife and blond meadow-sweet among
　　　　And darting swallows and light water-gnats,
　　　　　　We tracked the shy Thames shore?
　　Where are the mowers, who, as the tiny swell
　　　　Of our boat passing heaved the river-grass,
　　　　Stood with suspended scythe to see us pass?
They all are gone, and thou art gone as well!

Yes, thou art gone! and round me too the night
　　In ever-nearing circle weaves her shade.
　　　　I see her veil draw soft across the day,
　　I feel her slowly chilling breath invade
　　　　The cheek grown thin, the brown hair sprent with
　　　　　　grey;
　　　　　　I feel her finger light
　　Laid pausefully upon life's headlong train—
　　　　The foot less prompt to meet the morning dew,
　　　　The heart less bounding at emotion new,
And hope, once crushed, less quick to spring again.

And long the way appears, which seemed so short
　　To the less practised eye of sanguine youth;
　　　　And high the mountain-tops, in cloudy air,
　　The mountain-tops where is the throne of Truth,
　　　　Tops in life's morning-sun so bright and bare!
　　　　　　Unbreachable the fort
　　Of the long-battered world uplifts its wall;
　　　　And strange and vain the earthly turmoil grows,
　　　　And near and real the charm of thy repose,
And night as welcome as a friend would fall.

But hush! the upland hath a sudden loss
  Of quiet!—Look, adown the dusk hill-side,
    A troop of Oxford hunters going home,
  As in old days, jovial and talking, ride!
      From hunting with the Berkshire hounds they
        come.
      Quick! let me fly, and cross
  Into yon farther field!—'Tis done; and see,
    Backed by the sunset, which doth glorify
    The orange and pale violet evening-sky,
  Bare on its lonely ridge, the Tree! the Tree!

I take the omen! Eve lets down her veil,
  The white fog creeps from bush to bush about,
    The west unflushes, the high stars grow bright,
  And in the scattered farms the lights come out.
    I cannot reach the signal-tree to-night,
      Yet, happy omen, hail!
  Hear it from thy broad lucent Arno-vale
    (For there thine earth-forgetting eyelids keep
    The morningless and unawakening sleep
  Under the flowery oleanders pale)

Hear it, O Thyrsis, still our tree is there!
  Ah, vain! These English fields, this upland dim,
    These brambles pale with mist engarlanded,
  That lone, sky-pointing tree, are not for him;
    To a boon southern country he is fled,
      And now in happier air,
  Wandering with the great Mother's train divine
    (And purer or more subtle soul than thee,
    I trow, the mighty Mother doth not see)
  Within a folding of the Apennine,

Thou hearest the immortal chants of old!—
  Putting his sickle to the perilous grain
    In the hot cornfield of the Phrygian king,
  For thee the Lityerses-song again
    Young Daphnis with his silver voice doth sing;
      Sings his Sicilian fold,
  His sheep, his hapless love, his blinded eyes—
    And how a call celestial round him rang,
    And heavenward from the fountain-brink he sprang,
  And all the marvel of the golden skies.

There thou art gone, and me thou leavest here
  Sole in these fields! yet will I not despair.
    Despair I will not, while I yet descry
  Neath the mild canopy of English air
    That lonely tree against the western sky.
      Still, still these slopes, 'tis clear,
  Our Gipsy-Scholar haunts, outliving thee!
    Fields where soft sheep from cages pull the hay,
    Woods with anemones in flower till May,
  Know him a wanderer still; then why not me?

A fugitive and gracious light he seeks,
  Shy to illumine; and I seek it too.
    This does not come with houses or with gold,
  With place, with honor, and a flattering crew;
    'Tis not in the world's market bought and sold;
      But the smooth-slipping weeks
  Drop by, and leave its seeker still untired;
    Out of the heed of mortals he is gone,
    He wends unfollowed, he must house alone;
  Yet on he fares, by his own heart inspired.

Thou too, O Thyrsis, on like quest wast bound;
  Thou wanderedst with me for a little hour!
    Men gave thee nothing; but this happy quest,
  If men esteemed thee feeble, gave thee power,
    If men procured thee trouble, gave thee rest.
      And this rude Cumner ground,
Its fir-topped Hurst, its farms, its quiet fields,
  Here cam'st thou in thy jocund youthful time,
  Here was thine height of strength, thy golden
      prime!
And still the haunt beloved a virtue yields.

What though the music of thy rustic flute
  Kept not for long its happy, country tone;
    Lost it too soon, and learnt a stormy note
  Of men contention-tost, of men who groan,
    Which tasked thy pipe too sore, and tired by
      throat—
      It failed, and thou waste mute!
Yet hadst thou alway visions of our light,
  And long with men of care thou couldst not stay,
  And soon thy foot resumed its wandering way,
Left human haunt, and on alone till night.

Too rare, too rare, grow now my visits here!
  'Mid city-noise, not, as with thee of yore,
    Thyrsis! in reach of sheep-bells is my home.
  Then through the great town's harsh, heart-wearying
      roar,
    Let in thy voice a whisper often come,
      To chase fatigue and fear:

Why faintest thou? I wandered till I died.
  Roam on! The light we sought is shining still.
  Dost thou ask proof? Our tree yet crowns the
    hill,
Our Scholar travels yet the loved hill-side.

The Forsaken Merman

In this poem there are, as John Cowper Powys says,
"many stanzas that make you smell the salt foam, and
imagine all that lies, hidden and strange, down there upon
the glittering sand. That line

> *'Where great whales go sailing by,*
>   *Round the world forever and aye;'*

has a liberating power that may often recur when one is,
God knows, far enough from the spouting of any whale!
And the whole poem has a wistful, haunting beauty that
never grows tedious."

COME, dear children, let us away;
  Down and away below!
Now my brothers call from the bay,
Now the great winds shoreward blow,
Now the salt tides seaward flow;
Now the wild white horses play,
Champ and chafe and toss in the spray.
Children dear, let us away!
This way, this way!

Call her once before you go—
Call once yet!
In a voice that she will know:
"Margaret! Margaret!"

MATTHEW ARNOLD

Children's voices should be dear
(Call once more) to a mother's ear;
Children's voices, wild with pain—
Surely she will come again!
Call her once and come away;
This way, this way!
"Mother dear, we cannot stay!
The wild white horses foam and fret."
Margaret! Margaret!

Come, dear children, come away down;
Call no more!
One last look at the white-walled town,
And the little gray church on the windy shore,
Then come down!
She will not come though you call all day;
Come away, come away!

Children dear, was it yesterday
We heard the sweet bells over the bay?
In the caverns where we lay,
Through the surf and through the swell,
The far-off sound of a silver bell?
Sand-strewn caverns, cool and deep,
Where the winds are all asleep;
Where the spent lights quiver and gleam,
Where the salt weed sways in the stream,
Where the sea-beasts, ranged all round,
Feed in the ooze of their pasture-ground;
Where the sea-snakes coil and twine,
Dry their mail and bask in the brine;
Where great whales come sailing by,
Sail and sail, with unshut eye,
Round the world for ever and aye?

When did music come this way?
Children dear, was it yesterday?

Children dear, was it yesterday
(Call yet once) that she went away?
Once she sate with you and me,
On a red gold throne in the heart of the sea,
And the youngest sate on her knee.
She combed its bright hair, and she tended it well,
When down swung the sound of a far-off bell.
She sighed, she looked up through the clear green sea;
She said: "I must go, for my kinsfolk pray
In the little gray church on the shore to-day.
'Twill be Easter-time in the world—ah me!
And I lose my poor soul, Merman! here with thee."
I said: "Go up, dear heart, through the waves;
Say thy prayer, and come back to the kind sea-caves!"
She smiled, she went up through the surf in the bay.
Children dear, was it yesterday?

Children dear, were we long alone?
"The sea grows stormy, the little ones moan;
Long prayers," I said, "in the world they say;
Come!" I said; and we rose through the surf in the bay.
We went up the beach, by the sandy down
Where the sea-stocks bloom, to the white-walled town;
Through the narrow paved streets, where all was still,
To the little gray church on the windy hill.
From the church came a murmur of folk at their
　　　prayers,
But we stood without in the cold blowing airs.
We climbed on the graves, on the stones worn with
　　　rains,
And we gazed up the aisle through the small leaded
　　　panes.

She sate by the pillar; we saw her clear:
"Margaret, hist! come quick, we are here!
Dear heart," I said, "we are long alone;
The sea grows stormy, the little ones moan."
But, ah, she gave me never a look,
For her eyes were sealed to the holy book!
Loud prays the priest; shut stands the door.
Come away, children, call no more!
Come away, come down, call no more!

Down, down, down!
Down to the depths of the sea!
She sits at her wheel in the humming town,
Singing most joyfully.
Hark what she sings: "O joy, O joy,
For the humming street, and the child with its toy!
For the priest and the bell, and the holy well;
For the wheel where I spun,
And the blessed light of the sun!"
And so she sings her fill,
Singing most joyfully,
Till the spindle drops from her hand,
And the whizzing wheel stands still.
She steals to the window, and looks at the sand,
And over the sand at the sea;
And her eyes are set in a stare;
And anon there breaks a sigh,
And anon there drops a tear,
From a sorrow-clouded eye,
And a heart sorrow-laden,
A long, long sigh:
For the cold strange eyes of a little Mermaiden
And the gleam of her golden hair.

Come away, away children;
Come children, come down!
The hoarse wind blows coldly;
Lights shine in the town.
She will start from her slumber
When gusts shake the door;
She will hear the winds howling,
Will hear the waves roar.
We shall see, while above us
The waves roar and whirl,
A ceiling of amber,
A pavement of pearl.
Singing: "Here came a mortal,
But faithless was she!
And alone dwell for ever
The kings of the sea."

But, children, at midnight,
When soft the winds blow,
When clear falls the moonlight,
When spring tides are low;
When sweet airs come seaward
From heaths starred with broom,
And high rocks throw mildly
On the blanched sands a gloom;
Up the still, glistening beaches,
Up the creeks we will hie,
Over banks of bright seaweed
The ebb-tide leaves dry.
We will gaze, from the sand-hills,
At the white, sleeping town;
At the church on the hill-side—
And then come back down.
Singing: "There dwells a loved one,

But cruel is she!
She left lonely for ever
The kings of the sea."

The Burning of Balder's Ship

FROM "BALDER DEAD"

*Edmund Clarence Stedman says: "These fifty lines, which
describe the burning of Balder's ship—his funeral pyre—
have an imaginative grandeur rarely excelled in 'The
Idylls of the King.'"*

BUT now the sun had passed the height of Heaven,
  And soon had all that day been spent in wail;
But then the Father of the ages said:
    "Ye Gods, there well may be too much of wail!
Bring now the gathered wood to Balder's ship;
Heap on the deck the logs, and build the pyre."
    But when the Gods and Heroes heard, they brought
The wood to Balder's ship, and built a pile,
Full the deck's breadth, and lofty; then the corpse
Of Balder on the highest top they laid,
With Nanna on his right, and on his left
Hoder, his brother, whom his own hand slew.
And they set jars of wine and oil to lean
Against the bodies, and stuck torches near,
Splinters of pine-wood, soaked with turpentine;
And brought his arms and gold, and all his stuff,
And slew the dogs who at his table fed,
And his horse, Balder's horse, whom most he loved,
And placed them on the pyre, and Odin threw
A last choice gift thereon, his golden ring.
The mast they fixed, and hoisted up the sails,
Then they put fire to the wood; and Thor

Set his stout shoulder hard against the stern
To push the ship through the thick sand; sparks flew
From the deep trench she ploughed, so strong a God
Furrowed it; and the water gurgled in,
And the ship floated on the waves, and rocked.
But in the hills a strong east-wind arose,
And came down moaning to the sea; first squalls
Ran black o'er the sea's face, then steady rushed
The breeze, and filled the sails, and blew the fire.
And wreathed in smoke the ship stood out to sea.
Soon with a roaring rose the mighty fire,
And the pile crackled; and between the logs
Sharp quivering tongues of flame shot out, and leaped,
Curling and darting, higher, until they licked
The summit of the pile, the dead, the mast,
And ate the shrivelling sails; but still the ship
Drove on, ablaze above her hull with fire.
And the Gods stood upon the beach, and gazed.
And while they gazed, the sun went lurid down
Into the smoke-wrapt sea, and night came on.
Then the wind fell, with night, and there was calm;
But through the dark they watched the burning ship
Still carried o'er the distant waters on.
Farther and farther, like an eye of fire.
And long, in the far dark, blazed Balder's pile;
But fainter, as the stars rose high, it flared,
The bodies were consumed, ash choked the pile.
And as, in a decaying winter-fire,
A charred log, falling, makes a shower of sparks—
So with a shower of sparks the pile fell in,
Reddening the sea around; and all was dark.

But the Gods went by starlight up the shore
To Asgard, and sate down in Odin's hall
At table, and the funeral-feast began.

MATTHEW ARNOLD

Worldly Place

*E*VEN *in a palace, life may be led well!*
 So spake the imperial sage, purest of men,
Marcus Aurelius. But the stifling den
Of common life, where, crowded up pell-mell,
Our freedom for a little bread we sell,
And drudge under some foolish master's ken
Who rates us if we peer outside our pen—
Matched with a palace, is not this a hell?

Even in a palace! On his truth sincere,
Who spoke these words, no shadow ever came;
And when my ill-schooled spirit is aflame
Some nobler, ampler stage of life to win,
I'll stop, and say: "There were no succor here!
The aids to noble life are all within."

East London

'*T*WAS August, and the fierce sun overhead
 Smote on the squalid streets of Bethnal Green,
And the pale weaver, through his windows seen
In Spitalfields, looked thrice dispirited.
I met a preacher there I knew, and said:
"Ill and o'erworked, how fare you in this scene?"
"Bravely!" said he; "for I of late have been
Much cheered with thoughts of Christ, *the living bread.*"

O human soul! as long as thou canst so
Set up a mark of everlasting light,
Above the howling senses' ebb and flow,

To cheer thee, and to right thee if thou roam—
Not with lost toil thou laborest through the night!
Thou mak'st the heaven thou hop'st indeed thy home.

West London

CROUCHED on the pavement, close by Belgrave
        Square,
A tramp I saw, ill, moody and tongue-tied.
A babe was in her arms, and at her side
A girl; their clothes were rags, their feet were bare.
Some laboring men, whose work lay somewhere there,
Passed opposite; she touched her girl, who hied
Across, and begged, and came back satisfied.
The rich she had let pass with frozen stare.

Thought I: "Above her state this spirit towers;
She will not ask of aliens, but of friends,
Of sharers in a common human fate.
She turns from that cold succor, which attends
The unknown little from the unknowing great,
And points us to a better time than ours."

Morality

WE cannot kindle when we will
        The fire which in the heart resides;
The spirit bloweth and is still,
In mystery our soul abides.
    But tasks in hours of insight willed
    Can be through hours of gloom fulfilled.

With aching hands and bleeding feet
We dig and heap, lay stone on stone;
We bear the burden and the heat
Of the long day, and wish 'twere done.
 Not till the hours of light return
 All we have built do we discern.

Then, when the clouds are off the soul,
When thou dost bask in Nature's eye,
Ask, how *she* viewed thy self-control,
Thy struggling, tasked morality—
 Nature, whose free, light, cheerful air,
 Oft made thee, in thy gloom, despair.

Pis-Aller

MAN is blind because of sin,
 Revelation makes him sure;
Without that, who looks within,
Looks in vain, for all's obscure."

Nay, look closer into man!
Tell me, can you find indeed
Nothing sure, no moral plan
Clear prescribed, without your creed?

"No, I nothing can perceive!
Without that, all's dark for men.
That, or nothing, I believe."
For God's sake, believe it then!

MATTHEW ARNOLD

The Last Word

CREEP into thy narrow bed,
  Creep, and let no more be said!
Vain thy onset! all stands fast.
Thou thyself must break at last.

Let the long contention cease!
Geese are swans, and swans are geese.
Let them have it how they will!
Thou art tired; best be still.

They out-talked thee, hissed thee, tore thee?
Better men fared thus before thee;
Fired their ringing shot and passed,
Hotly charged—and sank at last.

Charge once more, then, and be dumb!
Let the victors, when they come,
When the forts of folly fall,
Find thy body by the wall!

WILLIAM BRIGHTY RANDS
ENGLAND, 1823-1880

The Thought

INTO the skies, one summer's day,
  I sent a little Thought away;
Up to where, in the blue round,
The sun sat shining without sound.

Then my Thought came back to me.
Little Thought, what did you see
In the regions whence you come?
And when I spoke, my Thought was dumb.

But she breathed of what was there,
In the pure bright upper air;
And, because my Thought so shone,
I knew she had been shone upon.

Next, by night a Thought I sent
Up into the firmament;
When the eager stars were out,
And the still moon shone about.

And my Thought went past the moon,
In between the stars, but soon
Held her breath and durst not stir,
For the fear that covered her;
Then she thought, in this demur:

"Dare I look beneath the shade,
Into where the worlds are made;
Where the suns and stars are wrought?
Shall I meet another Thought?

"Will that other Thought have wings?
Shall I meet strange, heavenly things?
Thought of Thoughts, and Light of Lights,
Breath of Breaths, and Night of Nights?"

Then my Thought began to hark
In the illuminated dark,
Till the silence, over, under,
Made her heart beat more than thunder.

And my Thought came trembling back,
But with something on her track,
And with something at her side;
Nor till she has lived and died,
Lived and died, and lived again,
Will that awful thing seem plain.

WILLIAM (JOHNSON) CORY
ENGLAND, 1823—1892

A Dirge

NAIAD, hid beneath the bank
    By the willowy river-side,
Where Narcissus gently sank,
    Where unmarried Echo died,
Unto thy serene repose
Waft the stricken Anteros.

Where the tranquil swan is borne,
    Imaged in a watery glass,
Where the sprays of fresh pink thorn
    Stoop to catch the boats that pass,
Where the earliest orchis grows,
Bury thou fair Anteros.

Glide we by, with prow and oar:
    Ripple shadows off the wave,
And reflected on the shore
    Haply play about his grave.
Folds of summer light enclose
All that once was Anteros.

On a flickering wave we gaze,
    Not upon his answering eyes:
Flower and bird we scarce can praise,
    Having lost his sweet replies:
Cold and mute the river flows
With our tears for Anteros.

COVENTRY PATMORE
ENGLAND, 1823-1896

PATMORE is the English laureate of Home and the Domestic Affections. His chief work is *The Angel in the House,* a narrative-reflective poem "for happy married people to read together, and to understand by the light of their own past and present life." For myself, I find *The Angel,* in the main, to be rather tedious reading. That poets like Tennyson and Browning, thinkers like Ruskin and Carlyle, should have accepted the work as a serious contribution to English poetry is declared by its detractors to be "one of the incomprehensible mysteries of criticism." On the other hand, Nathaniel Hawthorne calls it "a most beautiful and original poem"; and Alice Meynell finds in it "passages that are classic and very high in that noble rank. In depth of insight, energy of thought and intensity of descriptive power Patmore was rivalled only by Browning among his contemporaries."

Wasteful Woman

FROM "THE ANGEL IN THE HOUSE"

AH wasteful woman—she that may
  On her sweet self set her own price,
Knowing he cannot choose but pay—
  How has she cheapened Paradise!
How given for naught her priceless gift!
  How spoiled the bread and spilled the wine,
Which, spent with due respective thrift,
  Had made brutes men, and men divine!

COVENTRY PATMORE

Departure

IT was not like your great and gracious ways!
  Do you, that have naught other to lament,
Never, my Love, repent
Of how, that July afternoon,
You went,
With sudden, unintelligible phrase,
And frightened eye,
Upon your journey of so many days
Without a single kiss, or a good-bye?
I knew, indeed, that you were parting soon;
And so we sate, within the low sun's rays,
You whispering to me, for your voice was weak,
Your harrowing praise.
Well, it was well
To hear you such things speak,
And I could tell
What made your eyes a growing gloom of love,
As a warm South-wind sombres a March grove.
And it was like your great and gracious ways
To turn your talk on daily things, my Dear,
Lifting the luminous, pathetic lash
To let the laughter flash,
Whilst I drew near,
Because you spoke so low that I could scarcely hear.
But all at once to leave me at the last,
More at the wonder than the loss aghast,
With huddled, unintelligible phrase,
And frightened eye,
And go your journey of all days
With not one kiss, or a good-bye,
And the only loveless look the look with which you
    passed:
'Twas all unlike your great and gracious ways.

COVENTRY PATMORE

The Toys

FROM "THE UNKNOWN EROS"

MY little Son, who looked from thoughtful eyes
  And moved and spoke in quiet grown-up wise,
Having my law the seventh time disobeyed,
I struck him, and dismissed
With hard words and unkissed,
—His Mother, who was patient, being dead.
Then, fearing lest his grief should hinder sleep,
I visited his bed,
But found him slumbering deep,
With darkened eyelids, and their lashes yet
From his late sobbing wet.
And I, with moan,
Kissing away his tears, left others of my own;
For, on a table drawn beside his head,
He had put, within his reach,
A box of counters and a red-veined stone,
A piece of glass abraded by the beach,
And six or seven shells,
A bottle with bluebells,
And two French copper coins, ranged there with careful
    art,
To comfort his sad heart.
So when that night I prayed
To God, I wept, and said:
Ah, when at last we lie with trancèd breath,
Not vexing Thee in death,
And Thou rememberest of what toys
We made our joys,
How weakly understood
Thy great commanded good,

Then, fatherly not less
Than I whom Thou hast molded from the clay,
Thou'lt leave Thy wrath, and say,
"I will be sorry for their childishness."

Magna Est Veritas

*I include these lines because they express a popular fallacy
—the idea that Truth will win her victories without help
from men. The fact is that Truth wins her battles only by
the devotion and sacrifice of heroes. In her high historic
march, she travels only on the path of martyrdom. I try
to throw this idea upon the screen in my little poem, "The
Peril of Ease." Here is a stanza:*

*"The old-time heroes you honor, whose banners you bear,
  The whole world no longer prohibits;
 But if you peer into the past you will find them there,
  Swinging from gibbets."*

HERE, in this little Bay,
   Full of tumultuous life and great repose,
Where, twice a day,
The purposeless, glad ocean comes and goes,
Under high cliffs, and far from the huge town,
I sit me down.
For want of me the world's course will not fail;
When all its work is done, the lie shall rot;
The truth is great, and shall prevail,
When none cares whether it prevail or not.

SYDNEY DOBELL

ENGLAND, 1824-1874

DOBELL is fairly entitled to be considered an original poet, of a minor order. Shakespeare, Dryden, Burns, Byron and Browning may be said to descend from Chaucer, as Milton, Wordsworth, Shelley and Tennyson come down from Spenser. Dobell also is of the line and stock of Spenser. Few poets are so uneven, perhaps hardly any other capable of rising to high levels has ever sunk to such low levels. Many of his passages are mere fustian, some are outrages against all taste; but others have a sublimity not often surpassed.

How's My Boy?

HO, sailor of the sea!
    How's my boy—my boy?"
"What's your boy's name, good wife,
And in what good ship sailed he?"

"My boy John—
He that went to sea—
What care I for the ship, sailor?
My boy's my boy to me.

"You came back from sea,
And not know my John?
I might as well have asked some landsman,
Yonder down in the town.
There's not an ass in all the parish
But knows my John.

SYDNEY DOBELL

"How's my boy—my boy?
And unless you let me know
I'll swear you are no sailor,
Blue jacket or no—
Brass buttons or no, sailor,
Anchor and crown or no—
Sure his ship was the 'Jolly Briton' "—
"Speak low, woman, speak low!"

"And why should I speak low, sailor,
About my own boy John?
If I was loud as I am proud
I'd sing him over the town!
Why should I speak low, sailor?"—
"That good ship went down."

"How's my boy—my boy?
What care I for the ship, sailor—
I was never aboard her.
Be she afloat or be she aground,
Sinking or swimming, I'll be bound
Her owners can afford her!
I say, how's my John?"—
"Every man on board went down,
Every man aboard her."

"How's my boy—my boy?
What care I for the men, sailor?
I'm not their mother—
How's my boy—my boy?
Tell me of him and no other!
How's my boy—my boy?"

SYDNEY DOBELL

The Ballad of Keith of Ravelston

THE murmur of the mourning ghost
    That keeps the shadowy kine,
"O Keith of Ravelston,
    The sorrows of thy line!"

Ravelston, Ravelston,
    The merry path that leads
Down the golden morning hill,
    And through the silver meads;

Ravelston, Ravelston,
    The stile beneath the tree,
The maid that kept her mother's kine,
    The song that sang she!

She sang her song, she kept her kine,
    She sat beneath the thorn,
When Andrew Keith of Ravelston
    Rode through the Monday morn.

His henchmen sing, his hawk-bells ring,
    His belted jewels shine;
O Keith of Ravelston,
    The sorrows of thy line!

Year after year, where Andrew came,
    Comes evening down the glade,
And still there sits a moonshine ghost
    Where sat the sunshine maid.

Her misty hair is faint and fair,
　　She keeps the shadowy kine;
O Keith of Ravelston,
　　The sorrows of thy line!

I lay my hand upon the stile,
　　The stile is lone and cold,
The burnie that goes babbling by
　　Says naught that can be told.

Yet, stranger! here, from year to year,
　　She keeps her shadowy kine;
O Keith of Ravelston,
　　The sorrows of thy line!

Step out three steps, where Andrew stood—
　　Why blanch thy cheeks for fear?
The ancient stile is not alone,
　　'Tis not the burn I hear!

She makes her immemorial moan,
　　She keeps her shadowy kine;
"O Keith of Ravelston,
　　The sorrows of thy line!"

SYDNEY DOBELL

Monk's Song
From "The Roman"

THERE went an incense through the land one night,
    Through the hushed holy land, when tired men
        slept.   [*Interlude of music.*
The haughty sun of June had walked, long days,
Through the tall pastures which, like mendicants,
Hung their sere heads and sued for rain: and he
Had thrown them none. And now it was high hay-time,
Through the sweet valley all the flowery wealth
At once lay low, at once ambrosial blood
Cried to the moonlight from a thousand fields.
And through the land the incense went that night,
Through the hushed holy land when tired men slept.
  It fell upon the sage; who with his lamp
Put out the light of heaven. He felt it come
Sweetening the musty tomes, like the fair shape
Of that one blighted love, which from the past
Steals oft among his moldering thoughts of wisdom.
And SHE came with it, borne on airs of youth;
Old days sang round her, old memorial days;
She crowned with tears, they dressed in flowers, all
        faded—
And the night-fragrance is a harmony
All through the old man's soul. Voices of eld,
The home, the church upon the village green,
Old thoughts that circle like the birds of Even
Round the grey spire. Soft sweet regrets, like sunset
Lighting old windows with gleams day had not.
Ghosts of dead years, whispering old silent names
Through grass-grown pathways, by halls moldering
        now.

Childhood—the fragrance of forgotten fields;
Manhood—the unforgotten fields whose fragrance
Passed like a breath; the time of buttercups,
The fluttering time of sweet forget-me-nots;
The time of passion and the rose—the hay-time
Of that last summer of hope! The old man weeps,
The old man weeps.
His aimless hands the joyless books put by;
As one that dreams and fears to wake, the sage
With vacant eye stifles the trembling taper,
Lets in the moonlight—and for once is wise.

America

NOR force nor fraud shall sunder us! Oh ye
   Who north or south, on east or western land,
Native to noble sounds, say truth for truth,
Freedom for freedom, love for love, and God
For God: Oh ye who in eternal youth
Speak with a living and creative flood
This universal English, and do stand
Its breathing book, live worthy of that grand
Heroic utterance—parted, yet a whole,
Far, yet unsevered—children brave and free
Of the great Mother-tongue, and shall ye be
Lords of an Empire wide as Shakespeare's soul,
Sublime as Milton's immemorial theme,
And rich as Chaucer's speech, and fair as Spenser's
      dream.

SYDNEY DOBELL

Fragments from "Balder"

*In his poem "Balder", Dobell seeks to trace the progress
of a human being from Doubt to Faith, from Chaos to
Order. "Not," as the poet says, "of Doubt incarnate to
Faith incarnate, but of a doubtful mind to a faithful
mind." Taken as a whole, the poem is not a success, but
passages flash through it like meteors. By what a strong,
daring figure does Balder describe the elements of his
power!*

THOUGHT, Labor, Patience,
    And a strong Will, that, being set to boil
The broth of Hecate, would shred his flesh
Into the caldron, and stir deep, with arms
Flayed to the seething bone, ere there default
One tittle from the spell—these should not strive
In vain!

               The repose
Of Beauty—where she lieth bright and still
As some spent angel, dead-asleep in light
On the most heavenward top of all this world,
Wing-weary.

Of what follows death he says—

The first, last secret all men hear, and none
Betray.

            My hand shakes;
But with the trembling eagerness of him
Who buys an Indian kingdom with a bead.

Fancy, like the image that our boors
Set by their kine, doth milk her of her tears,
And loose the terrible unsolved distress
Of tumid Nature.

2132

SYDNEY DOBELL

Men of drug and scalpel still are men.
                    I call them the gnomes
Of science, miners who scarce see the light,
Working within the bowels of the world
Of beauty.

                    Love
Makes us all poets——
                    From the mount
Of high transfiguration you come down
Into your common lifetime, as the diver
Breathes upper air a moment ere he plunge,
And by mere virtue of that moment, lives
In breathless deeps, and dark. We poets live
Upon the height, saying, as one of old,
"Let us make tabernacles: it is good
To be here."

Sere leaf, that quiverest through the sad-still air;
Sere leaf, that waverest down the sluggish wind;
Sere leaf, that whirlest on the autumn gust,
Free in the ghastly anarchy of death:
The sudden gust that, like a headsman wild,
Uplifteth beauty by her golden hair,
To show the world that she is dead indeed.

                    The bare hill top
Shines near above us; I feel like a child
Nursed on his grandsire's knee, that longs to stroke
The bald bright forehead; shall we climb?

                    She looked in her surprise
As when the Evening Star, taken unaware,
While fearless she pursues across the Heaven

Her Lover-Sun, and on a sudden stands
Confessed in the pursuit, before a world
Upgazing, in her maiden innocence
Disarms us, and so looks, that she becomes
A worship evermore.

The ordered pomp and sacred dance of things.

This is that same hour
That I have seen before me as a star
Seen from a rushing comet through the black
And forward night, which orbs, and orbs, and orbs,
Till that which was a shining spot in space
Flames out between us and the universe,
And burns the heavens with glory.

WILLIAM ALLINGHAM
IRELAND, 1824–1889

ALLINGHAM is a spontaneous lyrist who was content to
err on the side of Nature rather than on that of Art,
and was more careful to keep his gift pure than to develop
it to the utmost. Not the least of his excellencies was
modesty. "The man has a true spirit of song in him,"
Tennyson wrote to Gladstone.

WILLIAM ALLINGHAM

The Fairies

UP the airy mountain,
  Down the rushy glen,
We daren't go a-hunting
  For fear of little men;
Wee folk, good folk,
  Trooping all together;
Green jacket, red cap,
  And white owl's feather!

Down along the rocky shore
  Some make their home,
They live on crispy pancakes
  Of yellow tide foam;
Some in the reeds
  Of the black mountain lake,
With frogs for their watch-dogs,
  All night awake.

High on the hill-top
  The old king sits;
He is now so old and gray
  He's nigh lost his wits.
With a bridge of white mist
  Columbkill he crosses,
On his stately journeys
  From Slieveleague to Rosses:

Or going up with music
  On cold starry nights,
To sup with the Queen
  Of the gay Northern lights.

They stole little Bridget
  For seven years long;
When she came down again
  Her friends were all gone.

They took her lightly back,
  Between the night and morrow,
They thought that she was fast asleep,
  But she was dead with sorrow.
They have kept her ever since
  Deep within the lake,
On a bed of flag-leaves,
  Watching till she wake.

By the craggy hill-side,
  Through the mosses bare,
They have planted thorn-trees
  For pleasure here and there.
Is any man so daring
  As dig them up in spite,
He shall find their sharpest thorns
  In his bed at night.

Up the airy mountain,
  Down the rushy glen,
We daren't go a-hunting
  For fear of little men;
Wee folk, good folk,
  Trooping all together;
Green jacket, red cap,
  And white owl's feather!

WILLIAM ALLINGHAM

Four Ducks on a Pond

FOUR ducks on a pond,
    A grass-bank beyond,
A blue sky of spring,
White clouds on the wing—
What a little thing
To remember for years. . . .
To remember with tears!

A Dream

I HEARD the dogs howl in the moon light night;
    I went to the window to see the sight;
All the Dead that ever I knew
Going one by one and two by two.

On they passed, and on they passed;
Townsfellows all, from first to last;
Born in the moonlight of the lane,
Quenched in the heavy shadow again.

Schoolmates, marching as when we played
At soldiers once—but now more staid;
Those were the strangest sight to me
Who were drowned, I knew, in the awful sea.

Straight and handsome folk; bent and weak, too;
Some that I loved, and gasped to speak to;
Some but a day in their churchyard bed;
Some that I had not known were dead.

A long, long crowd—where each seemed lonely,
Yet of them all there was one, one only,
Raised a head or looked my way:
She lingered a moment—she might not stay.

How long since I saw that fair pale face!
Ah! Mother dear! might I only place
My head on thy breast, a moment to rest,
While thy hand on my tearful cheek were prest!

On, on, a moving bridge they made
Across the moon-stream, from shade to shade,
Young and old, women and men;
Many long-forgot, but remembered then.

And first there came a bitter laughter;
A sound of tears the moment after;
And then a music so lofty and gay,
That every morning, day by day,
I strive to recall it—if I may.

GEORGE MACDONALD
SCOTLAND, 1824-1905

THIS Scotch poet and novelist abandoned the ministry for a literary career, publishing three volumes of poems and numerous novels. As a novelist he had a remarkable narrative and dramatic power, humor, tenderness, a genial view of life and character. Within his limits he was a true poet. To say something new about a lark, for instance, as Macdonald does in his *Song of the Lark,* is a feat. Yet here is the lark in character, freshly dramatized, suggestive, poignant.

The Song of the Lark

I WILL sing a song,
    I'm the Lark."
"Sing, sing, throat strong,
    Little kill-the-dark.
What will you sing about
Now the night is out?"

"I can only call;
    I can't think.
Let me up—that's all.
    Let me drink!
Thirsting all the long night
For a drink of light."

GEORGE MACDONALD

Martin Elginbrodde

HERE lie I, Martin Elginbrodde:
    Hae mercy o' my soul, Lord God,
As I wad do were I Lord God,
And ye were Martin Elginbrodde.

The Sweeper of the Floor

METHOUGHT that in a solemn church I stood.
    Its marble acres, worn with knees and feet,
Lay spread from door to door, from street to street.
Midway the form hung high upon the rood
Of Him who gave His life to be our good;
Beyond, priests flitted, bowed, and murmured meet,
Among the candles shining still and sweet.
Men came and went, and worshipped as they could—
And still their dust a woman with her broom,
Bowed to her work, kept sweeping to the door.
Then saw I, slow through all the pillared gloom,
Across the church a silent figure come:
"Daughter," it said, "thou sweepest well my floor!"
"It is the Lord!" I cried, and saw no more.

ADELAIDE ANNE PROCTER
ENGLAND, 1825–1864

A Woman's Question

BEFORE I trust my fate to thee,
  Or place my hand in thine,
Before I let thy future give
  Color and form to mine,
Before I peril all for thee,
Question thy soul to-night for me.

I break all slighter bonds, nor feel
  A shadow of regret:
Is there one link within the past
  That holds thy spirit yet?
Or is thy faith as clear and free
As that which I can pledge to thee?

Does there within thy dimmest dreams
  A possible future shine,
Wherein thy life could henceforth breathe,
  Untouched, unshared by mine?
If so, at any pain or cost,
Oh, tell me before all is lost!

Look deeper still: if thou canst feel,
  Within thy inmost soul,
That thou hast kept a portion back,
  While I have staked the whole:

Let no false pity spare the blow,
But in true mercy tell me so.

Is there within thy heart a need
    That mine cannot fulfill?
One chord that any other hand
    Could better wake or still?
Speak now, lest at some future day
My whole life wither and decay.

Lives there within thy nature hid
    The demon-spirit, change,
Shedding a passing glory still
    On all things new and strange?
It may not be thy fault alone.
But shield my heart against thine own.

Couldst thou withdraw thy hand one day
    And answer to my claim,
That fate, and that to-day's mistake,
    Not thou—had been to blame?
Some soothe their conscience thus; but thou
Wilt surely warn and save me now.

Nay, answer *not*—I dare not hear,
    The words would come too late;
Yet I would spare thee all remorse,
    So comfort thee, my fate:
Whatever on my heart may fall,
Remember, I *would* risk it all!

DINAH MULOCK CRAIK
ENGLAND, 1826—1887

Douglas, Douglas, Tender and True

COULD ye come back to me, Douglas, Douglas,
  In the old likeness that I knew,
I would be so faithful, so loving, Douglas,
  Douglas, Douglas, tender and true.

Never a scornful word should grieve ye,
  I'd smile on ye sweet as the angels do—
Sweet as your smile on me shone ever,
  Douglas, Douglas, tender and true.

O to call back the days that are not!
  My eyes were blinded, your words were few:
Do you know the truth now up in heaven,
  Douglas, Douglas, tender and true?

I never was worthy of you, Douglas—
  Not half worthy the like of you:
Now all men beside seem to me like shadows—
  I love *you*, Douglas, tender and true.

Stretch out your hand to me, Douglas, Douglas,
  Drop forgiveness from heaven like dew;
As I lay my heart on your dead heart, Douglas,
  Douglas, Douglas, tender and true.

GEORGE WALTER THORNBURY
England, 1828–1876

Here is a lyrist and balladist with flashes of fire and rushes of rhythm. He is sometimes hasty and coarse and unbridled, but you will find in his *Songs of the Cavaliers and Roundheads* fine gleams from the summit of his genius.

The Three Troopers

Into the Devil tavern
  Three booted troopers strode,
From spur to feather spotted and splashed
  With the mud of a winter road.
In each of their cups they dropped a crust,
  And stared at the guests with a frown:
Then drew their swords, and roared for a toast,
  "God send this Crum-well-down!"

A blue smoke rose from their pistol locks,
  Their sword blades were still wet:
There were long red smears on their jerkins of buff,
  As the table they overset.
Then into their cups they stirred the crusts,
  And cursed old London town:
Then waved their swords, and drank with a stamp,
  "God send this Crum-well-down!"

The 'prentice dropped his can of beer,
  The host turned pale as a clout:
The ruby nose of the toping squire

Grew white at the wild men's shout.
Then into their cups they flung the crusts
    And showed their teeth with a frown:
They flashed their swords as they gave the toast,
    "God send this Crum-well-down!"

The gambler dropped his dog's-eared cards,
    The waiting-women screamed,
As the light of the fire, like stains of blood,
    On the wild men's sabres gleamed:
Then into their cups they splashed the crusts,
    And cursed the fool of a town,
And leaped on the table, and roared a toast,
    "God send this Crum-well-down!"

Till on a sudden fire-bells rang,
    And the troopers sprang to horse:
The eldest muttered between his teeth,
    Hot curses—deep and coarse.
In their stirrup cups they flung the crusts,
    And cried as they spurred through town,
With their keen swords drawn and their pistols cocked,
    "God send this Crum-well-down!"

Away they dashed through Temple Bar,
    Their red cloaks flowing free,
Their scabbards clashed, each back-piece shone—
    None liked to touch the three.
The silver cups that held the crusts
    They flung to the startled town,
Shouting again, with a blaze of swords,
    "God send this Crum-well-down!"

GEORGE WALTER THORNBURY

The Jester's Sermon

THE Jester shook his hood and bells, and leaped
    upon a chair,
The pages laughed, the women screamed, and tossed
    their scented hair:
The falcon whistled, staghounds bayed, the lapdog
    barked without,
The scullion dropped the pitcher brown, the cook railed
    at the lout:
The steward, counting out his gold, let pouch and money
    fall,
And why? because the Jester rose to say grace in the
    hall!

The page played with the heron's plume, the steward
    with his chain,
The butler drummed upon the board, and laughed with
    might and main:
The grooms beat on their metal cans, and roared till
    they were red,
But still the Jester shut his eyes and rolled his witty
    head;
And when they grew a little still, read half a yard of
    text,
And, waving hand, struck on the desk, then frowned
    like one perplexed.

"Dear sinners all," the Fool began, "man's life is but a
    jest,
A dream, a shadow, bubble, air, a vapor at the best.
In a thousand pounds of law I find not a single ounce
    of love;

GEORGE WALTER THORNBURY

A blind man killed the parson's cow in shooting at the
  dove;
The fool that eats till he is sick must fast till he is well;
The wooer who can flatter most will bear away the
  belle.

"Let no man halloo he is safe till he is through the
  wood:
He who will not when he may, must tarry when he
  should;
He who laughs at crookèd men should need walk very
  straight:
Oh, he who once has won a name may lie abed till
  eight!
Make haste to purchase house and land, be very slow to
  wed:
True coral needs no painter's brush, nor need be daubed
  with red.

"The friar, preaching, cursed the thief (the pudding in
  his sleeve)
To fish for sprats with golden hooks is foolish, by your
  leave—
To travel well—an ass's ears, ape's face, hog's mouth,
  and ostrich legs:
He does not care a pin for thieves who limps about and
  begs.
Be always first man at a feast and last man at a fray:
The short way round, in spite of all, is still the longest
  way.
When the hungry curate licks the knife, there's not much
  for the clerk:
When the pilot, turning pale and sick, looks up—the
  storm grows dark."

Then loud they laughed, the fat cook's tears ran down
    into the pan:
The steward shook, that he was forced to drop the
    brimming can;
And then again the women screamed, and every stag-
    hound bayed—
And why? because the motley Fool so wise a sermon
    made.

La Tricoteuse

THE fourteenth of July had come,
    And round the guillotine
The thieves and beggars, rank by rank,
    Moved the red flags between.
A crimson heart, upon a pole—
    The long march had begun;
But still the little smiling child
    Sat knitting in the sun.

The red caps of those men of France
    Shook like a poppy-field:
Three women's heads, with gory hair,
    The standard-bearers wield.
Cursing, with song and battle-hymn,
    Five butchers dragged a gun;
Yet still the little maid sat there,
    A-knitting in the sun.

An axe was painted on the flags,
    A broken throne and crown,
A ragged coat, upon a lance;
    Hung in foul black shreds down.

"More heads!" the seething rabble cry,
  And now the drums begun;
But still the little fair-haired child
  Sat knitting in the sun.

And every time a head rolled off,
  They roll like winter seas;
And, with a tossing up of caps,
  Shouts shook the Tuileries.
Whizz—went the heavy chopper down,
  And then the drums begun;
But still the little smiling child
  Sat knitting in the sun.

The Jacobins, ten thousand strong,
  And every man a sword:
The red caps, with the tricolors,
  Led on the noisy horde.
"The *Sans Culottes* to-day are strong,"
  The gossips say, and run;
But still the little maid sits there,
  A-knitting in the sun.

Then the slow death-cart moved along;
  And, singing patriot songs,
A pale, doomed poet bowing comes
  And cheers the swaying throngs.
Oh, when the axe swept shining down,
  The mad drums all begun;
But, smiling still, the little child
  Sat knitting in the sun.

"*Le marquis*," linen snowy white,
  The powder in his hair,

Waving his scented handkerchief,
  Looks down with careless stare.
A whirr, a chop—another head—
  Hurrah! the work's begun;
But still the little child sat there,
  A-knitting in the sun.

A stir, and through the parting crowd
  The people's friends are come;
Marat and Robespierre—*"Vivat!*
  Roll thunder from the drum."
The one a wild beast's hungry eye,
  Hair tangled—hark! a gun!—
The other kindly kissed the child
  A-knitting in the sun.

"And why not work all night?" the child
  Said to the knitters there.
Oh how the furies shook their sides,
  And tossed their grizzled hair!
Then clapped a *bonnet rouge* on her,
  And cried, " 'Tis well begun!"
And laughed to see the little child
  Knit, smiling in the sun.

DANTE GABRIEL ROSSETTI
England, 1828-1882

DANTE GABRIEL ROSSETTI was a great creative artist, whose genius expressed itself felicitously on both page and canvas. Many departments of human activity had no existence for him. His reasoning powers were hardly beyond the average; but his instincts were unerring, and his perceptions keen and true.

I can recall no other great poem that has been so vastly improved by revision as *The Blessed Damozel*. It is an elegy that does not contain one single note of sorrow. It is perhaps the most complete vision of flesh and blood ever transported into the heavenly dominion. The arm of this Blessed Damozel warms the bar upon which she leans as she looks down from the sky to see her lover wandering forlorn on earth. Whether considered in itself as a cry of passionate spirituality, or as the work of a youth of eighteen or nineteen, it is a unique masterpiece.

In English literature Rossetti has a firm place as one of the six major poets of the later Victorian era and as a leader of the group of artists who brought about the revival known as Pre-Raphaelitism. He had an extraordinary faculty of packing a world of meaning into one pregnant and melodious phrase. He is at once the most spiritual and the most material of poets; and the accusation of sensuality from which he was made to suffer could only result from an inability to see more than one side of the Druid shield of his poetical personality.

DANTE GABRIEL ROSSETTI

The Blessed Damozel

THE blessed damozel leaned out
   From the gold bar of Heaven;
Her eyes were deeper than the depth
   Of waters stilled at even;
She had three lilies in her hand,
   And the stars in her hair were seven.

Her robe, ungirt from clasp to hem,
   No wrought flowers did adorn,
But a white rose of Mary's gift,
   For service meetly worn;
Her hair that lay along her back
   Was yellow like ripe corn.

Herseemed she scarce had been a day
   One of God's choristers;
The wonder was not yet quite gone
   From that still look of hers;
Albeit, to them she left, her day
   Had counted as ten years.

(To *one* it is ten years of years.
   . . . Yet now, and in this place,
Surely she leaned o'er me—her hair
   Fell all about my face. . . .
Nothing: the autumn fall of leaves.
   The whole year sets apace.)

It was the rampart of God's house
   That she was standing on;
By God built over the sheer depth
   The which is Space begun;

So high, that looking downward thence
   She scarce could see the sun.

It lies in Heaven, across the flood
   Of ether, as a bridge.
Beneath, the tides of day and night
   With flame and darkness ridge
The void, as low as where this earth
   Spins like a fretful midge.

Around her, lovers, newly met
   'Mid deathless love's acclaims,
Spoke evermore among themselves
   Their heart-remembered names;
And the souls mounting up to God
   Went by her like thin flames.

And still she bowed herself and stooped
   Out of the circling charm;
Until her bosom must have made
   The bar she leaned on warm,
And the lilies lay as if asleep
   Along her bended arm.

From the fixed place of Heaven she saw
   Time like a pulse shake fierce
Through all the worlds. Her gaze still strove
   Within the gulf to pierce
Its path; and now she spoke as when
   The stars sang in their spheres.

The sun was gone now; the curled moon
   Was like a little feather
Fluttering far down the gulf; and now

She spoke through the still weather.
Her voice was like the voice the stars
  Had when they sang together.

(Ah sweet! Even now, in that bird's song,
  Strove not her accents there,
Fain to be hearkened? When those bells
  Possessed the mid-day air,
Strove not her steps to reach my side
  Down all the echoing stair?)

"I wish that he were come to me,
  For he will come," she said.
"Have not I prayed in Heaven?—on earth,
  Lord, Lord, has he not prayed?
Are not two prayers a perfect strength?
  And shall I feel afraid?

"When round his head the aureole clings,
  And he is clothed in white,
I'll take his hand and go with him
  To the deep wells of light;
As unto a stream we will step down,
  And bathe there in God's sight.

"We two will stand beside that shrine,
  Occult, withheld, untrod,
Whose lamps are stirred continually
  With prayer sent up to God;
And see our old prayers, granted, melt
  Each like a little cloud.

"We two will lie i' the shadow of
  That living mystic tree
Within whose secret growth the Dove

2154

Is sometimes felt to be,
While every leaf that His plumes touch
    Saith His Name audibly.

"And I myself will teach to him,
    I myself, lying so,
The songs I sing here; which his voice
    Shall pause in, hushed and slow,
And find some knowledge at each pause,
    Or some new thing to know."

(Alas! we two, we two, thou say'st!
    Yea, one wast thou with me
That once of old. But shall God lift
    To endless unity
The soul whose likeness with thy soul
    Was but its love for thee?)

"We two," she said, "will seek the groves
    Where the lady Mary is,
With her five handmaidens, whose names
    Are five sweet symphonies,
Cecily, Gertrude, Magdalen,
    Margaret and Rosalys.

"Circlewise sit they, with bound locks
    And foreheads garlanded;
Into the fine cloth white like flame
    Weaving the golden thread,
To fashion the birth-robes for them
    Who are just born, being dead.

"He shall fear, haply, and be dumb:
    Then will I lay my cheek
To his, and tell about our love,

Not once abashed or weak:
And the dear Mother will approve
    My pride, and let me speak.

"Herself shall bring us, hand in hand,
    To Him round whom all souls
Kneel, the clear-ranged unnumbered heads
    Bowed with their aureoles;
And angels meeting us shall sing
    To their citherns and citoles.

"There will I ask of Christ the Lord
    Thus much for him and me:
Only to live as once on earth
    With Love, only to be,
As then awhile, for ever now
    Together, I and he."

She gazed and listened and then said,
    Less sad of speech than mild:
"All this is when he comes." She ceased.
    The light thrilled towards her, filled
With angels in strong level flight.
    Her eyes prayed, and she smiled.

(I saw her smile.) But soon their path
    Was vague in distant spheres:
And then she cast her arms along
    The golden barriers,
And laid her face between her hands,
    And wept. (I heard her tears.)

DANTE GABRIEL ROSSETTI

The Sonnet

A SONNET is a moment's monument—
   Memorial from the Soul's eternity
To one dead deathless hour. Look that it be,
Whether for lustral rite or dire portent,
Of its own arduous fulness reverent:
   Carve it in ivory or in ebony,
   As Day or Night may rule; and let Time see
Its flowering crest impearled and orient.

A Sonnet is a coin: its face reveals
   The soul—its converse, to what Power 'tis due:
Whether for tribute to the august appeals
   Of Life, or dower in Love's high retinue,
It serve; or, 'mid the dark wharf's cavernous breath,
In Charon's palm it pay the toll to Death.

From "The House of Life"

*At times, Rossetti can be charged with hard and tortuous
expression: he then lacks the direct and driving utterance
of his namesake Dante. I have selected nine of his flawless sonnets. There is nothing else like "The House of Life"
in English poetry; and we read with deep interest Swinburne's eulogy of the sonnet sequence: "This 'House of
Life' has in it so many mansions, so many halls of state
and bowers of music, chapels for worship and chambers
for festival, that no guest can declare on a first entrance
the secret of its scheme."*
*This winged eulogy flies on and on to tell how in these
sonnets we find "the birth of Love, his eucharistic presence,*

*his supreme vision, his utter union in flesh and spirit, the
secret of the sanctuary of his heart, his louder music and
his lower, his graver and his lighter seasons: all work of
Love and all play, all dreams and devices of his memory
and his belief, all fuller and emptier hours from the first
which longs for him to the last which loses, all change of
lights from his midday to his moonrise, all his foreknowl-
edge of evil things and good, all glad and sad hours of his
nightwatchers, all agonies and consolations that embitter
and allay the wounds of his mortal hour . . . and beyond
all the light of the unaccomplished hour which missed its
chance in one life to meet it in another where the sundered
spirits revive into reunion."*

LOVE ENTHRONED

I MARKED all kindred Powers the heart finds
    fair:
Truth, with awed lips; and Hope, with eyes upcast;
And Fame, whose loud wings fan the ashen Past
To signal-fires, Oblivion's flight to scare;
And Youth, with still some single golden hair
Unto his shoulder clinging, since the last
Embrace wherein two sweet arms held him fast;
And Life, still wreathing flowers for Death to wear.

Love's throne was not with these; but far above
All passionate wind of welcome and farewell
He sat in breathless bowers they dream not of;
Though Truth foreknow Love's heart, and Hope fore-
    tell,
And Fame be for Love's sake desirable,
And Youth be dear, and Life be sweet to Love.

DANTE GABRIEL ROSSETTI

BRIDAL BIRTH

A S when desire, long darkling, dawns, and first
The mother looks upon the new-born child,
Even so my Lady stood at gaze and smiled
When her soul knew at length the Love it nursed.
Born with her life, creature of poignant thirst
And exquisite hunger, at her heart Love lay
Quickening in darkness, till a voice that day
Cried on him, and the bonds of birth were burst.

Now, shadowed by his wings, our faces yearn
Together, as his fullgrown feet now range
The grove, and his warm hands our couch prepare:
Till to his song our bodiless souls in turn
Be born his children, when Death's nuptial change
Leaves us for light the halo of his hair.

LOVESIGHT

W HEN do I see thee most, belovèd one?
When in the light the spirits of mine eyes
Before thy face, their altar, solemnize
The worship of that Love through thee made known?
Or when in the dusk hours (we two alone)
Close-kissed and eloquent of still replies—
Thy twilight-hidden glimmering visage lies,
And my soul only sees thy soul its own?

O Love, my Love! if I no more should see
Thyself, nor on the earth the shadow of thee,
Nor image of thine eyes in any spring—
How then should sound upon Life's darkening slope
The ground-whirl of the perished leaves of Hope,
The wind of Death's imperishable wing?

DANTE GABRIEL ROSSETTI

HEART'S HOPE

BY what word's power, the key of paths untrod,
  Shall I the difficult deeps of love explore.
Till parted waves of Song yield up the shore
Even as that sea which Israel crossed dryshod?
For lo! in some poor rhythmic period,
  Lady, I fain would tell how evermore
  Thy soul I know not from thy body, nor
Thee from myself, neither our love from God.

Yea, in God's name, and Love's, and thine, would I
  Draw from one loving heart such evidence
As to all hearts all things shall signify;
  Tender as dawn's first hill-fire, and intense
  As instantaneous penetrating sense,
In Spring's birth-hour, of other Springs gone by.

THE DARK GLASS

NOT I myself know all my love for thee:
  How should I reach so far, who cannot weigh
To-morrow's dower by gage of yesterday?
Shall birth and death, and all dark names that be
As doors and windows bared to some loud sea,
  Lash deaf mine ears and blind my face with spray;
  And shall my sense pierce love—the last relay
And ultimate outpost of eternity?

Lo! what am I to Love, the lord of all?
  One murmuring shell he gathers from the sand—
  One little heart-flame sheltered in his hand.
Yet through thine eyes he grants me clearest call
And veriest touch of powers primordial
  That any hour-girt life may understand.

TRUE WOMAN—HER HEAVEN

IF to grow old in Heaven is to grow young,
  (As the Seer saw and said) then blest were he
With youth for evermore, whose heaven should be
True Woman, she whom these weak notes have sung,
Here and hereafter—choir-strains of her tongue—
  Sky-spaces of her eyes—sweet signs that flee
  About her soul's immediate sanctuary—
Were Paradise all uttermost worlds among.

The sunrise blooms and withers on the hill
  Like any hillflower; and the noblest troth
  Dies here to dust. Yet shall Heaven's promise clothe
Even yet those lovers who have cherished still
  This test for love: in every kiss sealed fast
  To feel the first kiss and forbode the last.

SOUL'S BEAUTY

(*Sibylla Palmifera*)

UNDER the arch of Life, where love and death,
  Terror and mystery, guard her shrine, I saw
  Beauty enthroned; and though her gaze struck awe
I drew it in as simply as my breath.
Hers are the eyes which, over and beneath,
  The sky and sea bend on thee—which can draw,
  By sea or sky or woman, to one law,
The allotted bondman of her palm and wreath.

This is that Lady Beauty, in whose praise
  Thy voice and hand shake still; long known to thee
  By flying hair and fluttering hem—the beat
Following her daily of thy heart and feet,

How passionately and irretrievably,
In what fond flight, how many ways and days!

BODY'S BEAUTY

OF Adam's first wife, Lilith, it is told
    (The witch he loved before the gift of Eve)
  That, ere the snake's, her sweet tongue could deceive,
And her enchanted hair was the first gold.
And still she sits, young while the earth is old,
    And, subtly of herself contemplative,
  Draws men to watch the bright web she can weave,
Till heart and body and life are in its hold.

The rose and poppy are her flowers: for where
  Is he not found, O Lilith! whom shed scent
And soft-shed kisses and soft sleep shall snare?
  Lo! as that youth's eyes burned at thine, so went
  Thy spell through him, and left his straight neck bent,
And round his heart one strangling golden hair.

A SUPERSCRIPTION

LOOK in my face; my name is Might-have-been;
    I am also called No-more, Too-late, Farewell;
  Unto thine ear I hold the dead-sea shell
Cast up thy Life's foam-fretted feet between;
Unto thine eyes the glass where that is seen
    Which had Life's form and Love's, but by my spell
  Is now a shaken shadow intolerable,
Of ultimate things unuttered the frail screen.

Mark me, how still I am! But should there dart
  One moment through thy soul the soft surprise
  Of that winged Peace which lulls the breath of
    sighs—

Then shalt thou see me smile, and turn apart
Thy visage to mine ambush at thy heart
  Sleepless with cold commemorative eyes.

One Girl (*A Combination from "Sappho"*)

I

LIKE the sweet apple which reddens upon the top-
    most bough,
A-top on the topmost twig—which the pluckers for-
    got, somehow—
Forgot it not, nay, but got it not, for none could get it
    till now.

II

Like the wild hyacinth flower which on the hills is
    found,
Which the passing feet of the shepherds for ever tear
    and wound,
Until the purple blossom is trodden into the ground.

Sister Helen

WHY did you melt your waxen man,
                    Sister Helen?
Today is the third since you began."
"The time was long, yet the time ran,
                    Little brother,"
        (*O Mother, Mary Mother,*
Three days today, between Hell and Heaven!)

"But if you have done your work aright,
                    Sister Helen,
You'll let me play, for you said I might."
"Be very still in your play tonight,
                    Little brother,"
            (*O Mother, Mary Mother,*
Third night, tonight, between Hell and Heaven!)

"You said it must melt ere vesper-bell,
                    Sister Helen;
If now it be molten, all is well."
"Even so—nay, peace! you cannot tell,
                    Little brother,"
            (*O Mother, Mary Mother,*
O what is this, between Hell and Heaven?)

"Oh the waxen knave was plump to-day,
                    Sister Helen;
How like dead folk he has dropped away!"
"Nay now, of the dead what can you say,
                    Little brother?"
            (*O Mother, Mary Mother,*
What of the dead, between Hell and Heaven?)

"See, see, the sunken pile of wood,
                    Sister Helen,
Shines through the thinned wax red as blood!"
"Nay now, when looked you yet on blood,
                    Little brother?"
            (*O Mother, Mary Mother,*
How pale she is, between Hell and Heaven!)

"Now close your eyes, for they're sick and sore,
                    Sister Helen,
And I'll play without the gallery door."

"Aye, let me rest—I'll lie on the floor,
                    Little brother,"
              (*O Mother, Mary Mother,*
What rest tonight, between Hell and Heaven?)

"Here high up in the balcony,
                    Sister Helen,
The moon flies face to face with me."
"Aye, look and say whatever you see,
                    Little brother,"
              (*O Mother, Mary Mother,*
What sight tonight, between Hell and Heaven?)

"Outside it's merry in the wind's wake,
                    Sister Helen,
In the shaken trees the chill stars shake."
"Hush, heard you a horse-tread as you spake,
                    Little brother?"
              (*O Mother, Mary Mother,*
What sound tonight, between Hell and Heaven?)

"I hear a horse-tread, and I see,
                    Sister Helen,
Three horsemen that ride terribly."
"Little brother, whence come the three,
                    Little brother?"
              (*O Mother, Mary Mother,*
Whence should they come, between Hell and Heaven?)

"They come by the hill-verge from Boyne Bar,
                    Sister Helen,
And one draws nigh, but two are afar."

"Look, look, do you know them who they are,
                              Little brother?"
                    (*O Mother. Mary Mother,*
Who should they be, between Hell and Heaven?)

"Oh, it's Keith of Eastholm rides so fast,
                              Sister Helen,
For I know the white mane on the blast."
"The hour has come, has come at last,
                              Little brother!"
                    (*O Mother, Mary Mother,*
Her hour at last, between Hell and Heaven!)

"He has made a sign and called Halloo!
                              Sister Helen,
And he says that he would speak with you."
"Oh tell him I fear the frozen dew,
                              Little brother."
                    (*O Mother, Mary Mother,*
Why laughs she thus, between Hell and Heaven!)

"The wind is loud, but I hear him cry.
                              Sister Helen.
That Keith of Ewern's like to die."
"And he and thou, and thou and I,
                              Little brother."
                    (*O Mother, Mary Mother,*
And they and we, between Hell and Heaven!)

"Three days ago, on his marriage-morn,
                              Sister Helen,
He sickened, and lies since then forlorn."

"For bridegroom's side is the bride a thorn,
                        Little brother?"
                    (*O Mother, Mary Mother,*
Cold bridal cheer, between Hell and Heaven!)

"Three days and nights he has lain abed,
                        Sister Helen,
And he prays in torment to be dead."
"The thing may chance, if he have prayed,
                        Little brother!"
                    (*O Mother, Mary Mother,*
If he have prayed, between Hell and Heaven!)

"But he has not ceased to cry to-day,
                        Sister Helen,
That you should take your curse away."
"My prayer was heard—he need but pray
                        Little brother!"
                    (*O Mother, Mary Mother,*
Shall God not hear, between Hell and Heaven?)

"But he says, till you take back your ban,
                        Sister Helen,
His soul would pass, yet never can."
"Nay then, shall I slay a living man,
                        Little brother?"
                    (*O Mother, Mary Mother,*
A living soul, between Hell and Heaven!)

"But he calls for ever on your name,
                        Sister Helen,
And says that he melts before a flame."
"My heart for his pleasure fared the same,
                        Little brother."
                    (*O Mother, Mary Mother,*
Fire at the heart, between Hell and Heaven!)

"Here's Keith of Westholm riding fast,
                        Sister Helen,
For I know the white plume on the blast."
"The hour, the sweet hour I forecast,
                        Little brother!"
                        (*O Mother, Mary Mother,*
Is the hour sweet, between Hell and Heaven?)

"He stops to speak, and he stills his horse,
                        Sister Helen;
But his words are drowned in the wind's course."
"Nay hear, nay hear, you must hear perforce,
                        Little brother!"
                        (*O Mother, Mary Mother,*
What word now heard, between Hell and Heaven?)

"Oh he says that Keith of Ewern's cry,
                        Sister Helen,
Is ever to see you ere he die."
"In all that his soul sees, there am I,
                        Little brother!"
                        (*O Mother, Mary Mother,*
The soul's one sight, between Hell and Heaven!)

"He sends a ring and a broken coin,
                        Sister Helen,
And bids you mind the banks of Boyne."
"What else he broke will he ever join,
                        Little brother?"
                        (*O Mother, Mary Mother,*
No, never joined, between Hell and Heaven!)

"He yields you these and craves full fain,
                        Sister Helen,

You pardon him in his mortal pain."
'What else he took will he give again,
>> Little brother?"
>>> (*O Mother, Mary Mother,*
Not twice to give, between Hell and Heaven!)

"He calls your name in an agony,
>> Sister Helen,
That even dead Love must weep to see."
"Hate, born of Love, is blind as he,
>> Little brother!"
>>> (*O Mother, Mary Mother,*
Love turned to hate, between Hell and Heaven!)

"Oh it's Keith of Keith now that rides fast,
>> Sister Helen,
For I know the white hair on the blast."
"The short, short hour will soon be past,
>> Little brother!"
>>> (*O Mother, Mary Mother,*
Will soon be past, between Hell and Heaven!)

"He looks at me and he tries to speak,
>> Sister Helen,
But oh! his voice is sad and weak!"
"What here should the mighty Baron seek,
>> Little brother?"
>>> (*O Mother, Mary Mother,*
Is this the end, between Hell and Heaven?)

"Oh his son still cries, if you forgive,
>> Sister Helen,
The body dies, but the soul shall live."

"Fire shall forgive me as I forgive,
                    Little brother!"
                (*O Mother, Mary Mother,*
As she forgives, between Hell and Heaven!)

"Oh he prays you, as his heart would rive,
                    Sister Helen,
To save his dear son's soul alive."
"Fire cannot slay it, it shall thrive,
                    Little brother!"
                (*O Mother, Mary Mother,*
Alas, alas, between Hell and Heaven!)

"He cries to you, kneeling in the road,
                    Sister Helen,
To go with him for the love of God!"
"The way is long to his son's abode,
                    Little brother."
                (*O Mother, Mary Mother,*
The way is long, between Hell and Heaven!)

"A lady's here, by a dark steed brought,
                    Sister Helen,
So darkly clad, I saw her not."
"See her now or never see aught,
                    Little brother!"
                (*O Mother, Mary Mother,*
What more to see, between Hell and Heaven?)

"Her hood falls back, and the moon shines fair,
                    Sister Helen,
On the Lady of Ewern's golden hair."

"Blest hour of my power and her despair,
                Little brother!"
                    (O Mother, Mary Mother,
Hour blest and banned, between Hell and Heaven!)

"Pale, pale her cheeks, that in pride did glow,
                Sister Helen,
'Neath the bridal-wreath three days ago."
"One morn for pride and three days for woe.
                Little brother!"
                    (O Mother, Mary Mother,
Three days, three nights, between Hell and Heaven!)

"Her clasped hands stretch from her bending head,
                Sister Helen;
With the loud wind's wail her sobs are wed."
"What wedding-strains hath her bridal-bed,
                Little brother?"
                    (O Mother, Mary Mother,
What strain but death's, between Hell and Heaven?)

"She may not speak, she sinks in a swoon,
                Sister Helen;
She lifts her lips and gasps on the moon."
"Oh! might I but hear her soul's blithe tune,
                Little brother!"
                    (O Mother, Mary Mother,
Her woe's dumb cry, between Hell and Heaven!)

"They've caught her to Westholm's saddle-bow,
                Sister Helen,
And her moonlit hair gleams white in its flow."

"Let it turn whiter than winter snow,
                    Little brother!"
            (*O Mother, Mary Mother,*
Woe-withered gold, between Hell and Heaven!)

"O Sister Helen, you heard the bell,
                    Sister Helen!
More loud than the vesper-chime it fell."
"No vesper-chime, but a dying knell,
                    Little brother!"
            (*O Mother, Mary Mother,*
His dying knell, between Hell and Heaven!)

"Alas! but I fear the heavy sound,
                    Sister Helen;
Is it in the sky or in the ground?"
"Say, have they turned their horses round,
                    Little brother?"
            (*O Mother, Mary Mother,*
What would she more, between Hell and Heaven?)

"They have raised the old man from his knee,
                    Sister Helen,
And they ride in silence hastily."
"More fast the naked soul doth flee,
                    Little brother!"
            (*O Mother, Mary Mother,*
The naked soul, between Hell and Heaven!)

"Flank to flank are the three steeds gone,
                    Sister Helen,
But the lady's dark steed goes alone."
"And lonely her bridegroom's soul hath flown,
                    Little brother."
            (*O Mother, Mary Mother,*
The lonely ghost, between Hell and Heaven!)

"Oh the wind is sad in the iron chill,
                                        Sister Helen,
And weary sad they look by the hill."
"But he and I are sadder still,
                                        Little brother!"
                        (*O Mother, Mary Mother,*
Most sad of all, between Hell and Heaven!)

"See, see, the wax has dropped from its place,
                                        Sister Helen,
And the flames are winning up apace!"
"Yet here they burn but for a space,
                                        Little brother!"
                        (*O Mother, Mary Mother,*
Here for a space, between Hell and Heaven!)

"Ah! what white thing at the door has crossed,
                                        Sister Helen?
Ah! what is this that sighs in the frost?"
"A soul that's lost as mine is lost,
                                        Little brother!"
                        (*O Mother, Mary Mother,*
Lost, lost, all lost, between Hell and Heaven!)

The Portrait

THIS is her picture as she was:
    It seems a thing to wonder on,
As though mine image in the glass
    Should tarry when myself am gone.
I gaze until she seems to stir—
Until mine eyes almost aver
    That now, even now, the sweet lips part

To breathe the words of the sweet heart:
And yet the earth is over her.

Alas! even such the thin-drawn ray
  That makes the prison-depths more rude—
The drip of water night and day
    Giving a tongue to solitude.
Yet this, of all love's perfect prize,
Remains; save what in mournful guise
  Takes counsel with my soul alone—
  Save what is secret and unknown,
Below the earth, above the skies.

In painting her I shrined her face
  Mid mystic trees, where light falls in
Hardly at all; a covert place
  Where you may think to find a din
Of doubtful talk, and a live flame
Wandering, and many a shape whose name
  Not itself knoweth, and old dew,
  And your own footsteps meeting you,
And all things going as they came.

A deep dim wood; and there she stands
  As in that wood that day: for so
Was the still movement of her hands
  And such the pure line's gracious flow.
And passing fair the type must seem,
Unknown the presence and the dream.
  'Tis she: though of herself, alas!
  Less than her shadow on the grass
Or than her image in the stream.

That day we met there, I and she
  One with the other all alone;

And we were blithe; yet memory
   Saddens those hours, as when the moon
Looks upon daylight. And with her
I stooped to drink the spring-water,
   Athirst where other waters sprang;
   And where the echo is, she sang—
My soul another echo there.

But when that hour my soul won strength
   For words whose silence wastes and kills,
Dull raindrops smote us, and at length
   Thundered the heat within the hills.
That eve I spoke those words again
Beside the pelted window-pane;
   And there she hearkened what I said,
   With under-glances that surveyed
The empty pastures blind with rain.

Next day the memories of these things,
   Like leaves through which a bird has flown,
Still vibrated with Love's warm wings;
   Till I must make them all my own
And paint this picture. So, 'twixt ease
Of talk and sweet long silences,
   She stood among the plants in bloom
   At windows of a summer room,
To feign the shadow of the trees.

And as I wrought, while all above
   And all around was fragrant air,
In the sick burthen of my love
   It seemed each sun-thrilled blossom there
Beat like a heart among the leaves.
O heart that never beats nor heaves,

In that one darkness lying still,
    What now to thee my love's great will
Or the fine web the sunshine weaves?

For now doth daylight disavow
    Those days—nought left to see or hear.
Only in solemn whispers now
    At night-time these things reach mine ear,
When the leaf shadows at breath
Shrink in the road, and all the heath,
    Forest and water, far and wide,
    In limpid starlight glorified,
Lie like the mystery of death.

Last night at last I could have slept,
    And yet delayed my sleep till dawn,
Still wandering. Then it was I wept:
    For unawares I came upon
Those glades where once she walked with me;
And as I stood there suddenly,
    All wan with traversing the night,
    Upon the desolate verge of light
Yearned loud the iron-bosomed sea.

Even so, where Heaven holds breath and hears
    The beating heart of Love's own breast—
Where round the secret of all spheres
    All angels lay their wings to rest—
How shall my soul stand rapt and awed,
When, by the new birth borne abroad
    Throughout the music of the suns,
    It enters in her soul at once
And knows the silence there for God!

Here with her face doth memory sit
  Meanwhile, and wait the day's decline,
Till other eyes shall look from it,
  Eyes of the spirit's Palestine,
Even than the old gaze tenderer;
While hopes and aims long lost with her
  Stand round her image side by side,
  Like tombs of pilgrims that have died
About the Holy Sepulchre.

Two English Poets

THOMAS CHATTERTON

WITH Shakespeare's manhood at a boy's wild
    heart—
Through Hamlet's doubt to Shakespeare near allied,
And kin to Milton through his Satan's pride—
At Death's sole door he stooped, and craved a dart;
And to the dear new bower of England's art—
  Even to that shrine Time else had deified,
  The unuttered heart that soared against his side,
Drove the fell point, and smote life's seals apart.

Thy nested home-loves, noble Chatterton;
  The angel-trodden stair thy soul could trace
  Up Redcliffe's spire: and in the world's armed space
Thy gallant sword-play: these to many an one
Are sweet for ever; as thy grave unknown
  And love-dream of thine unrecorded face.

DANTE GABRIEL ROSSETTI

WILLIAM BLAKE

(To Frederick Shields, on his Sketch of Blake's work-room
and death-room, 3 Fountain Court, Strand.)

THIS is the place. Even here the dauntless soul,
  The unflinching hand, wrought on; till in that
      nook,
As on that very bed, his life partook
New birth, and passed. Yon river's dusky shoal,
Whereto the close-built coiling lanes unroll,
  Faced his work-window, whence his eyes would stare,
  Thought-wandering, unto nought that met them
      there,
But to the unfettered irreversible goal.

This cupboard, Holy of Holies, held the cloud
  Of his soul writ and limned; this other one,
His true wife's charge, full oft to their abode
  Yielded for daily bread the martyr's stone,
  Ere yet their food might be that Bread alone,
The words now home-speech of the mouth of God.

The Sea-Limits

CONSIDER the sea's listless chime:
  Time's self it is, made audible—
  The murmur of the earth's own shell.
Secret continuance sublime
  Is the sea's end: our sight may pass
  No furlong further. Since time was,
This sound hath told the lapse of time.

No quiet, which is death's—it hath
  The mournfulness of ancient life,
  Enduring always at dull strife.
As the world's heart of rest and wrath,
  Its painful pulse is in the sands.
  Last utterly, the whole sky stands,
Gray and not known, along its path.

Listen alone beside the sea,
  Listen alone among the woods;
  Those voices of twin solitudes
Shall have one sound alike to thee:
  Hark where the murmurs of thronged men
  Surge and sink back and surge again—
Still the one voice of wave and tree.

Gather a shell from the strown beach
  And listen at its lips: they sigh
  The same desire and mystery,
The echo of the whole sea's speech.
  And all mankind is thus at heart
  Not anything but what thou art:
And Earth, Sea, Man, are all in each.

Sudden Light

I HAVE been here before,
  But when or how I cannot tell:
I know the grass beyond the door,
  The sweet keen smell,
The sighing sound, the lights around the shore.

You have been mine before—
    How long ago I may not know:
But just when at that swallow's soar
    Your neck turned so,
Some veil did fall—I knew it all of yore.

Has this been thus before?
    And shall not thus time's eddying flight
Still with our lives our loves restore
    In death's despite,
And day and night yield one delight once more?

GEORGE MEREDITH
ENGLAND, 1828-1909

RANKED as a great English novelist, Meredith is also a distinguished poet of imagination and passion, although not a natural singer. His steps are often clogged and clodded. The first duty of a singer is to sing: Meredith seldom sings, but gives us abundant philosophy coupled with accurate nature detail. At his best, however —as in *Love in the Valley*—Meredith is often a consummate artist. His first volume of verse was published in 1851, followed eleven years later by *Modern Love,* probably his highest and most durable poetic achievement.

"The casual reader," says Richard Le Galliene, "looks upon Meredith's poems as chaos illuminated by flashes of lightning. But Meredith's obscurity, like Browning's, is not merely a result of grammatical compression. It is the more compound expression of endless metaphor. . . . 'Image treads upon image.'"

As literary adviser to a London publishing house, Meredith helped develop many young authors by his wise and kindly criticism. Thomas Hardy in particular has said that he probably would have never persevered in the path of literature without the encouragement given him by Meredith when he submitted his first manuscript.

Meredith's poetry came slowly into public notice and approval. His novels called attention to his poems long published without remark. Imbedded in his poetry we find his gritty philosophy. He, too, felt the spiritual tumult ushered in by the scientific revelations of Darwin and Wallace, the inescapable biological truth not then found compatible with scriptural affirmation. His God is manifest as eternal Law, and future progress to Meredith means the progress of mankind rather than the persistence of the soul beyond death.

This problem of immortality has never greatly troubled me. I am more amazed by the fact that *I am here* at all than by the idea of persisting after I change worlds. Meredith, however, has moments of inspiration in which his dark vision is dispelled by hope. Into a rather commonplace song, *The Spirit of Earth in Autumn,* he flings this beautiful thing:

> "Into the breast that gives the rose
> Shall I with shuddering fall?"

And here is another flash of intuition:

> "Cold as a mountain in its star-pitched tent
> Stood high philosophy, less friend than foe;
> Whom self-caged passion from its prison bars,
> Is always watching with a wondering hate.
> Not till the fire is dying in the grate
> Look we for any kinship with the stars."

Gilbert Chesterton sums the philosophy of Meredith in three illuminating sentences: "Meredith really is a Pantheist. You can express it by saying that God is the great All: you can express it more intelligently by saying that Pan is the great god. But there is some sense in it, and the sense is this: that some people believe that this world is sufficiently good at bottom for us to trust ourselves to it without very much knowing why."

GEORGE MEREDITH

Song in the Songless

THEY have no song, the sedges, dry,
  And still they sing.
It is within my breast they sing,
  As I pass by.
Within my breast they touch a string,
  They wake a sigh.
There is but sound of sedges dry;
  In me they sing.

Lucifer in Starlight

ON a starred night Prince Lucifer uprose.
  Tired of his dark dominion swung the fiend
Above the rolling ball in cloud part screened,
Where sinners hugged their spectre of repose.
Poor prey to his hot fit of pride were those.
  And now upon his western wing he leaned,
  Now his huge bulk o'er Afric's sands careened,
Now the black planet shadowed Arctic snows.

Soaring through wider zones that pricked his scars
  With memory of the old revolt from Awe,
He reached a middle height, and at the stars,
Which are the brain of heaven, he looked, and sank.
Around the ancient track marched, rank on rank,
  The army of unalterable law.

GEORGE MEREDITH

The Question Whither

WHEN we have thrown off this old suit,
  So much in need of mending,
To sink among the naked mute,
  Is that, you think, our ending?
We follow many, more we lead,
  And you who sadly turf us,
Believe not that all living seed
  Must flower above the surface.

Sensation is a gracious gift,
  But were it cramped to station,
The prayer to have it cast adrift,
  Would sprout from all sensation.
Enough if we have winked to sun,
  Have sped the plow in season:
There is a soul for labor done,
  Endureth fixed as reason.

Then let our trust be firm in Good,
  Though we be of the fasting;
Our questions are a mortal brood,
  Our work is everlasting.
We children of Beneficence
  Are in its being sharers:
And Whither vainer sounds than Whence,
  For word with such wayfarers.

GEORGE MEREDITH

Will o' the Wisp

FOLLOW me, follow me,
  Over brake and under tree,
Through the bosky tanglery,
        Brushwood and bramble.
  Follow me, follow me,
        Laugh and leap and scramble
  Follow, follow,
  Hill and hollow,
  Foss and burrow,
  Fen and furrow,
Down into the bulrush-beds,
Midst the reeds and osier-heads,
In the rushy, soaking damps,
Where the vapors pitch their camps,
    Follow me, follow me,
        For a midnight ramble!
Oh, what a mighty fog!
What a merry night O ho!
Follow, follow, nigher, nigher—
Over bank and pond and brier,
Down into the croaking ditches.
    Rotten log,
    Spotted frog,
    Beetle bright
    With crawling light,
        What a joy O ho!
Deep into the purple bog—
        What a joy O ho!
Where like hosts of puckered witches
All the shivering agues sit,
Warming hands and chafing feet,
By the blue marsh-hovering oils:

O the fools for all their moans!
Not a forest mad with fire
Could still their teeth, or warm their bones,
Or loose them from their chilly coils.
    What a clatter!
    How they chatter!
    Shrink and huddle,
    All a muddle,
        What a joy O ho!
Down we go, down we go,
        What a joy O ho!
Soon shall I be down below,
Plunging with a gray fat friar,
Hither, thither, to and fro,
        What a joy O ho!
Breathing mists and whisking lamps,
Plashing in the slimy swamps;
        What a joy O ho!
While my cousin Lantern Jack,
With cock ears and cunning eyes,
Turns him round upon his back,
Daubs him oozy green and black,
Sits upon his rolling size,
Where he lies, where he lies,
Groaning full of sack—
Staring with his great round eyes!
        What a joy O ho!
Sits upon him in the swamps,
Breathing mists and whisking lamps!
        What a joy O ho!
Such a lad is Lantern Jack,
When he rides the black nightmare
Through the fens, and puts a glare
In the friar's track.
Such a frolic lad, good lack!

To turn a friar on his back,
Trip him, clip him, whip him, nip him,
Lay him sprawling, smack!
Such a lad is Lantern Jack!
Such a tricksy lad, good lack!
What a joy O ho!
Follow me, follow me,
Where he sits, and you shall see!

The Spirit of Shakespeare

*There are two or three clodded spots in these two sonnets.
Nevertheless, I include them because the earnest comment
of one great soul upon another great soul is always worthy
of our attention.*

I

THY greatest knew thee, Mother Earth; unsoured
    He knew thy sons. He probed from hell to hell
Of human passions, but of love deflowered
His wisdom was not, for he knew thee well.
Thence came the honeyed corner at his lips,
The conquering smile wherein his spirit sails
Calm as the God who the white sea-wave whips,
Yet full of speech and intershifting tales,
Close mirrors of us: thence had he the laugh
We feel is thine: broad as ten thousand beeves
At pasture! thence thy songs, that winnow chaff
From grain, bid sick Philosophy's last leaves
Whirl, if they have no response—they enforced
To fatten Earth when from her soul divorced.

II

How smiles he at a generation ranked
In gloomy noddings over life! They pass.
Not he to feed upon a breast unthanked,
Or eye a beauteous face in a cracked glass.
But he can spy that little twist of brain
Which moved some weighty leader of the blind,
Unwitting 'twas the goad of personal pain,
To view in curst eclipse our Mother's mind,
And show us of some rigid harridan
The wretched bondmen till the end of time.
Oh, lived the Master now to paint us Man,
That little twist of brain would ring a chime
Of whence it came and what it caused, to start
Thunders of laughter, clearing air and heart.

From "*Modern Love*"

I

BY this he knew she wept with waking eyes:
   That, at his hand's light quiver by her head,
The strange low sobs that shook their common bed
Were called into her with a sharp surprise,
And strangled mute, like little gaping snakes,
Dreadfully venomous to him. She lay
Stone-still, and the long darkness flowed away
With muffled pulses. Then as midnight makes
Her giant heart of Memory and Tears
Drink the pale drug of silence, and so beat
Sleep's heavy measure, they from head to feet

Were moveless, looking through their dead black years,
By vain regret scrawled over the blank wall.
Like sculptured effigies they might be seen
Upon their marriage-tomb, the sword between;
Each wishing for the sword that severs all.

XVI

In our old shipwrecked days there was an hour,
When in the firelight steadily aglow,
Joined slackly, we beheld the red chasm grow
Among the clicking coals. Our library-bower
That eve was left to us: and hushed we sat
As lovers to whom Time is whispering.
From sudden-opened doors we heard them sing:
The nodding elders mixed good wine with chat.
Well knew we that Life's greatest treasure lay
With us, and of it was our talk. "Ah, yes!
Love dies!" I said: I never thought it less.
She yearned to me that sentence to unsay.
Then when the fire domed blackening, I found
Her cheek was salt against my kiss, and swift
Up the sharp scale of sobs her breast did lift—
Now am I haunted by that taste! that sound!

XLVII

We saw the swallows gathering in the sky,
And in the osier-isle we heard their noise.
We had not to look back on summer joys,
Or forward to a summer of bright dye:
But in the largeness of the evening earth
Our spirits grew as we went side by side.
The hour became her husband and my bride.
Love that had robbed us so, thus blessed our dearth!

The pilgrims of the year waxed very loud
In multitudinous chatterings, as the flood
Full brown came from the West, and like pale blood
Expanded to the upper crimson cloud.
Love that had robbed us of immortal things,
This little moment mercifully gave,
Where I had seen across the twilight wave
The swan sail with her young beneath her wings.

XLIX

He found her by the ocean's moaning verge,
Nor any wicked change in her discerned;
And she believed his old love had returned,
Which was her exultation, and her scourge.
She took his hand, and walked with him, and seemed
The wife he sought, though shadow-like and dry.
She had one terror, lest her heart should sigh,
And tell her loudly she no longer dreamed.
She dared not say, "This is my breast: look in."
But there's a strength to help the desperate weak.
That night he learned how silence best can speak
The awful things when Pity pleads for Sin.
About the middle of the night her call
Was heard, and he came wondering to the bed.
"Now kiss me, dear! it may be, now!" she said.
Lethe had passed those lips, and he knew all.

L

Thus piteously Love closed what he begat:
The union of this ever-diverse pair!
These two were rapid falcons in a snare,
Condemned to do the flitting of the bat.
Lovers beneath the singing sky of May,

GEORGE MEREDITH

They wandered once; clear as the dew on flowers:
But they fed not on the advancing hours:
Their hearts held cravings for the buried day.
Then each applied to each that fatal knife,
Deep questioning, which probes to endless dole.
Ah, what a dusty answer gets the soul
When hot for certainties in this our life!—
In tragic hints here see what evermore
Moves dark as yonder midnight ocean's force,
Thumping like ramping hosts of warrior horse,
To throw that faint thin line upon the shore!

Dirge in Woods

A WIND sways the pines,
      And below
Not a breath of wild air;
Still as the mosses that glow
On the flooring and over the lines
Of the roots here and there
The pine-tree drops its dead;
They are quiet as under the sea.
Overhead, overhead
Rushes life in a race,
As the clouds the clouds chase;
      And we go.
And we drop like the fruits of the tree,
      Even we,
      Even so.

GEORGE MEREDITH

From "Love in the Valley"

UNDER yonder beech-tree single on the green-
    sward,
  Couched with her arms behind her golden head,
Knees and tresses folded to slip and ripple idly,
  Lies my young Love sleeping in the shade.
Had I the heart to slide an arm beneath her,
  Press her parting lips as her waist I gather slow,
Waking in amazement she could not but embrace me:
  Then would she hold me and never let me go?

Shy as the squirrel and wayward as the swallow,
  Swift as the swallow along the river's light
Circleting the surface to meet his mirrored winglets,
  Fleeter she seems in her stay than in her flight.
Shy as the squirrel that leaps among the pine-tops,
  Wayward as the swallow overhead at set of sun,
She whom I love is hard to catch and conquer,
  Hard, but O the glory of the winning were she won!

When her mother tends her before the laughing mirror,
  Tying up her laces, looping up her hair.
Often she thinks, were this wild thing wedded,
  More love should I have, and much less care.
When her mother tends her before the lighted mirror,
  Loosening her laces, combing down her curls,
Often she thinks, were this wild thing wedded,
  I should miss but one for many boys and girls.

Heartless she is as the shadow in the meadows
  Flying to the hills on a blue and breezy noon.
No, she is athirst and drinking up her wonder:
  Earth to her is young as the slip of the new moon.
Deals she an unkindness, 'tis but her rapid measure,

Even as in a dance; and her smile can heal no less:
Like the swinging May-cloud that pelts the flowers with
    hailstones
  Off a sunny border, she was made to bruise and bless.

Lovely are the curves of the white owl sweeping
  Wavy in the dusk lit by one large star.
Lone on the fir-branch, his rattle-note unvaried,
  Brooding o'er the gloom, spins the brown evejar.
Darker grows the valley, more and more forgetting:
  So were it with me if forgetting could be willed.
Tell the grassy hollow that holds the bubbling well-
    spring,
  Tell it to forget the source that keeps it filled.

Stepping down the hill with her fair companions,
  Arm in arm, all against the raying West,
Boldly she sings, to the merry tune she marches,
  Brave is her shape, and sweeter unpossessed.
Sweeter, for she is what my heart first awaking
  Whispered the world was; morning light is she.
Love that so desires would fain keep her changeless;
  Fain would fling the net, and fain have her free.

Happy happy time, when the white star hovers
  Low over dim fields fresh with bloomy dew,
Near the face of dawn, that draws athwart the darkness,
  Threading it with color, like yewberries the yew.
Thicker crowd the shades as the grave East deepens
  Glowing, and with crimson a long cloud swells.
Maiden still the morn is; and strange she is, and secret;
  Strange her eyes; her cheeks are cold as cold sea-
    shells.

Sunrays, leaning on our southern hills and lighting
   Wild cloud-mountains that drag the hills along,
Oft ends the day of your shifting brilliant laughter
   Chill as a dull face frowning on a song.
Ay, but shows the South-west a ripple-feathered bosom
   Blown to silver while the clouds are shaken and
     ascend
Scaling the mid-heavens as they stream, there comes a
     sunset
   Rich, deep like love in beauty without end.

When at dawn she sighs, and like an infant to the
     window
   Turns grave eyes craving light, released from dreams,
Beautiful she looks, like a white water-lily
   Bursting out of bud in havens of the streams.
When from bed she rises clothed from neck to ankle
   In her long nightgown sweet as boughs of May,
Beautiful she looks, like a tall garden-lily
   Pure from the night, and splendid for the day.

Mother of the dews, dark eye-lashed twilight,
   Low-lidded twilight, o'er the valley's brim,
Rounding on thy breast sings the dew-delighted skylark,
   Clear as though the dewdrops had their voice in him.
Hidden where the rose-flush drinks the rayless planet,
   Fountain-full he pours the spraying fountain-showers.
Let me hear her laughter, I would have her ever
   Cool as dew in twilight, the lark above the flowers.

All the girls are out with their baskets for the primrose;
   Up lanes, woods through, they troop in joyful bands.
My Sweet leads: she knows not why, but now she loiters,
   Eyes the bent anemones, and hangs her hands.
Such a look will tell that the violets are peeping,

Coming the rose: and unaware a cry
Springs in her bosom for odors and for color,
  Covert and the nightingale; she knows not why.

Kerchiefed head and chin she darts between her tulips,
  Streaming like a willow gray in arrowy rain:
Some bend beaten cheek to gravel, and their angel
  She will be; she lifts them, and on she speeds again.
Black the driving raincloud breasts the iron gateway:
  She is forth to cheer a neighbor lacking mirth.
So when sky and grass met rolling dumb for thunder
  Saw I once a white dove, sole light of earth.

Prim little scholars are the flowers of her garden,
  Trained to stand in rows, and asking if they please.
I might love them well but for loving more the wild
    ones:
  O my wild ones! they tell me more than these.
You, my wild one, you tell of honied field-rose,
  Violet, blushing eglantine in life; and even as they,
They by the wayside are earnest of your goodness,
  You are of life's, on the banks that line the way.

Peering at her chamber the white crowns the red rose,
  Jasmine winds the porch with stars two and three.
Parted is the window; she sleeps; the starry jasmine
  Breathes a falling breath that carries thoughts of me.
Sweeter unpossessed, have I said of her my sweetest?
  Not while she sleeps: while she sleeps the jasmine
    breathes,
Luring her to love; she sleeps; the starry jasmine
  Bears me to her pillow under white rose-wreaths.

Yellow with birdfoot-trefoil are the grass-glades;
  Yellow with cinquefoil of the dew-gray leaf;

GEORGE MEREDITH

Yellow with stonecrop; the moss-mounds are yellow;
   Blue-necked the wheat sways, yellowing to the sheaf.
Green-yellow, bursts from the copse the laughing yaffle;
   Sharp as a sickle is the edge of shade and shine:
Earth in her heart laughs looking at the heavens,
   Thinking of the harvest: I look and think of mine.

This I may know: her dressing and undressing
   Such a change of light shows as when the skies in
      sport
Shift from cloud to moonlight; or edging over thunder
   Slips a ray of sun; or sweeping into port
White sails furl; or on the ocean borders
   White sails lean along the waves leaping green.
Visions of her shower before me, but from eyesight
   Guarded she would be like the sun were she seen.

Front door and back of the mossed old farmhouse
   Open with the morn, and in a breezy link
Freshly sparkles garden to stripe-shadowed orchard,
   Green across a rill where on sand the minnows wink.
Busy in the grass the early sun of summer
   Swarms, and the blackbird's mellow fluting notes
Call my darling up with round and roguish challenge:
   Quaintest, richest carol of all the singing throats!

Cool was the woodside; cool as her white dairy
   Keeping sweet the cream-pan; and there the boys from
      school,
Cricketing below, rushed brown and red with sunshine;
   O the dark translucence of the deep-eyed cool!
Spying from the farm, herself she fetched a pitcher
   Full of milk, and tilted for each in turn the beak.

Then a little fellow, mouth up and on tiptoe,
  Say, "I will kiss you": she laughed and leaned her
    cheek.

Doves of the fir-wood walling high our red roof
  Through the long noon coo, crooning through the coo.
Loose droop the leaves, and down the sleepy roadway
  Sometimes pipes a chaffinch, loose droops the blue.
Cows flap a slow tail knee-deep in the river,
  Breathless, given up to sun and gnat and fly.
Nowhere is she seen; and if I see her nowhere,
  Lightning may come, straight rains and tiger sky.

O the golden sheaf, the rustling treasure-armful!
  O the nutbrown tresses nodding interlaced!
O the treasure-tresses one another over
  Nodding! O the girdle slack about the waist!
Slain are the poppies that shot their random scarlet
  Quick amid the wheat-ears: wound about the waist,
Gathered, see these brides of Earth one blush of ripe-
    ness!
  O the nutbrown tresses nodding interlaced!

Large and smoky red the sun's cold disk drops,
  Clipped by naked hills, on violet shaded snow:
Eastward large and still lights up a bower of moonrise,
  Whence at her leisure steps the moon aglow.
Nightlong on black print-branches our beech-tree
  Gazes in this whiteness: nightlong could I.
Here may life on death or death on life be painted.
  Let me clasp her soul to know she cannot die!

Gossips count her faults; they scour a narrow chamber
  Where there is no window, read not heaven or her.
'When she was a tiny,' one agèd woman quavers,

Plucks at my heart and leads me by the ear.
Faults she had once as she learned to run and tumbled:
    Faults of feature some see, beauty not complete.
Yet, good gossips, beauty that makes holy
    Earth and air, may have faults from head to feet.

Hither she comes; she comes to me; she lingers,
    Deepens her brown eyebrows, while in new surprise
High rise the lashes in wonder of a stranger;
    Yet am I the light and living of her eyes.
Something friends have told her fills her heart to brimming,
    Nets her in her blushes, and wounds her, and tames.—
Sure of her haven, O like a dove alighting,
    Arms up, she dropped: our souls were in our names.

From "The Woods of Westermain"

"The woods of Westermain are the mysterious woods of Nature, whose spirit no man can interpret unless he enter the woods with courage and love," explains G. M. Trevelyan, adding: "Nature turns horrible to those who fear or carp at her."

I

ENTER these enchanted woods
    You who dare.
Nothing harms beneath the leaves
More than waves a swimmer cleaves.
Toss your heart up with the lark,
Foot at peace with mouse and worm,
    Fair you fare.

Only at a dread of dark
Quaver, and they quit their form:
Thousand eyeballs under hoods
    Have you by the hair.
Enter these enchanted woods,
    You who dare.

II

Here the snake across your path
Stretches in his golden bath:
Mossy-footed squirrels leap
Soft as winnowing plumes of Sleep:
Yaffles on a chuckle skim
Low to laugh from branches dim:
Up the pine, where sits the star,
Rattles deep the moth-winged jar:
Each has business of his own;
But should you mistrust a tone,
    Then beware.
Shudder all the haunted roods,
All the eyeballs under hoods
    Shroud you in their glare.
Enter these enchanted woods,
    You who dare.

GERALD MASSEY
ENGLAND, 1828–1907

From "Tale of Eternity"

*This poem deals finely with the problem of sin, the rela-
tionship of soul and body, and the influence of the spiritual
upon material life. It is full of poetic thought and spiritual
suggestion. A brief quotation must suffice.*

BOTH heaven and hell are from the human race,
   And every soul projects its future place;
Long shadows of ourselves are thrown before,
To wait our coming on the Eternal shore.
These either clothe us with eclipse and night,
Or, as we enter them, are lost in light.

*   *   *   *   *

No seed of life blown down a dark abysm
Of earth or sea but feels the magnetism
That draws us Godward! Flowers sunk in mines,
Or plants in ocean, where no sunbeam shines,
Will blindly climb up toward their Deity,
Far off in Heaven, whom they can never see.

There is a Spirit of Life within the Tree
That's fed and clothed from Heaven continually,
And does not draw all nourishment from earth.
It puts a myriad tender feelers forth,
That breathe in heaven and turn the breath to sap:
In every leaf it spreads a tiny lap

2200

To take its manna from the hand of God,
And gather force for fingers 'neath the sod
To clutch the earth with; molds, from sun and rain,
Its leaves; with spirit-life feeds every vein,
And through each vein makes wood for bough and bark:
Girth for the bole, and rootage down the dark.

So Man is fed by God and lives in Him:
Not merely nourished by his rootage dim
In a far Past; a dead world underground,
But spirit to spirit reaches life all round.

* * * * *

Not in one primal Man before the Fall
Did God set life a-breathing once for all,
He is the breath of life from first to last;
He liveth in the Present as the Past.

* * * * *

God hath been gradually forming Man
In His own image since the world began,
And is for ever working on the soul,
Like Sculptor on his Statue, till the whole
Expression of the upward life be wrought
Into some semblance of the Eternal Thought.
Race after Race hath caught its likeness of
The Maker as the eyes grew large with love.

GERALD MASSEY

The Captain of the Northfleet

SO often is the proud deed done
   By men like this at Duty's call;
So many are the honors won
   For us, we cannot wear them all!

They make the heroic common-place
   And dying thus the natural way;
And yet, our world-wide English race
   Feels nobler, for that death, To-day!

It stirs us with a sense of wings
   That strive to lift the earthiest soul;
It brings the thoughts that fathom things
   To anchor fast where billows roll.

Love was so new, and life so sweet,
   But at the call he left the wine,
And sprang full-statured to his feet,
   Responsive to the touch divine.

"Nay, Dear, I cannot see you die.
   For me, I have my work to do
Up here. Down to the boat. Good-bye,
   God bless you. I shall see it through."

We read, until the vision dims
   And drowns; but, ere the pang be past,
A tide of triumph overbrims
   And breaks with light from Heaven at last.

Through all the blackness of that night
   A glory streams from out the gloom;

GERALD MASSEY

His steadfast spirit lifts the light
　　That shines till Night is overcome.

The sea will do its worst, and life
　　Be sobbed out in a bubbling breath;
But firmly in the coward strife
　　There stands a man who has conquered Death.

A soul that masters wind and wave,
　　And towers above a sinking deck;
A bridge across the gaping grave;
　　A rainbow rising o'er the wreck.

Others he saved; he saved the name
　　Unsullied that he gave his wife:
And dying with so pure an aim,
　　He had no need to save his life!

Lord, how they shame the life we live,
　　These Sailors of our sea-girt isle,
Who cheerily take what Thou mayst give,
　　And go down with a heavenward smile!

The men who sow their lives to yield
　　A glorious crop in lives to be:
Who turn to England's Harvest-field
　　The unfruitful furrows of the sea.

With such a breed of men so brave,
　　The Old Land has not had her day;
But long, her strength, with crested wave,
　　Shall ride the Seas, the proud old way.

GERALD MASSEY

To-day and To-morrow

HIGH hopes that burned like stars-sublime,
　　Go down i' the heaven of freedom;
And true hearts perish in the time
　　We bitterliest need 'em!
But never sit we down and say
　　There's nothing left but sorrow;
We walk the wilderness to-day—
　　The promised land to-morrow!

Our birds of song are silent now,
　　Few are the flowers blooming,
Yet life is in the frozen bough,
　　And freedom's spring is coming;
And freedom's tide creeps up alway,
　　Though we may strand in sorrow;
And our good bark aground to-day,
　　Shall float again to-morrow.

'Tis weary watching wave by wave,
　　And yet the Tide heaves onward;
We climb, like Corals, grave by grave,
　　That pave a pathway sunward;
We are driven back, for our next fray
　　A newer strength to borrow,
And where the Vanguard camps To-day
　　The Rear shall rest To-morrow!

Through all the long, dark night of years
　　The people's cry ascendeth,
And earth is wet with blood and tears:
　　But our meek sufferance endeth!

GERALD MASSEY

The few shall not for ever sway—
    The many moil in sorrow;
The powers of hell are strong to-day,
    The Christ shall rise to-morrow!

Though hearts brood o'er the past, our eyes
    With smiling futures glisten!
For lo! our day bursts up the skies,
    Lean out your souls and listen!
The world is rolling freedom's way,
    And ripening with her sorrow;
Take heart! who bear the Cross to-day
    Shall wear the Crown to-morrow!

O youth! flame-earnest, still aspire
    With energies immortal!
To many a heaven of desire
    Our yearning opes a portal;
And though age wearies by the way,
    And hearts break in the furrow—
Youth sows the golden grain to-day—
    The harvest comes to-morrow!

Build up heroic lives, and all
    Be like a sheathen sabre,
Ready to flash out at God's call—
    O chivalry of labor!
Triumph and toil are twins; though they
    Be singly born in sorrow,
And 'tis the martyrdom to-day
    Brings victory to-morrow!

ALEXANDER SMITH

ENGLAND, 1829—1867

ALEXANDER SMITH was a protégé of the learned Scotch critic, George Gilfillan. His first work, *A Life Drama,* made, in its hour, a great sensation, one of the biggest ever staged by a young writer. His name was lifted beside even the names of Keats and Tennyson. Overrated then, he is now equally neglected. Almost wholly forgotten, in fact, is this man who said modestly:

> "I've learned to prize the quiet lightning deed,
> Not the applauding thunder at its heels,
> Which men call Fame."

Smith's characteristic was a superabundance of imagery, frequently splashing over into bathos. He is capable of a drop like this:

> "My heart is in the grave with her,
> The family went abroad."

He sometimes touches the horrible, by uniting the terrible with the disgusting: take this,

> "As holds the wretched West the sunset's corpse."

He seldom achieves simplicity—the fusing of thought and image into one inevitable unity. However, Smith has left us a few fragments of rich beauty and power. He speaks of someone:

> "As gaily dight
> As goldfinch swinging on a thistle-top."

Take also this couplet:

> "The marigold was burning in the marsh,
> Like a thing dipped in sunset."

Here is a well-rounded and vivid passage from his *Edwin of Deira*. Wordsworth, by the way, has a sonnet on this same theme from the Anglo-Saxon.

> "The sparrow flies
> In at one door, and by another out,
> Brief space of warm and comfortable air,
> It knows in passing, then it vanishes
> Into the gusty dark from whence it came.
> The soul like that same sparrow comes and goes:
> This life is but a moment's sparrow-flight
> Between the two unknowns of birth and death:
> An arrow's passage from an unknown bow
> Toward an unknown bourne."

A Quaint Character
FROM "A LIFE DRAMA"

I'LL show you one who might have been an abbot
In the old time; a large and portly man,
With merry eyes, and crown that shines like glass.
No thin-smiled April he, bedript with tears,
But appled-Autumn, golden-cheeked and tan;
A jest in his mouth feels sweet as crusted wine.
As if all eager for a merry thought,
The pits of laughter dimple in his cheeks.
His speech is flavorous, evermore he talks
In a warm, brown, autumnal sort of style.

ALEXANDER SMITH

The King Dying on the Battle-Field

Here is a sterner and loftier strain, flashing with the epic imagination.

THE grim old king,
    Whose blood leaped madly when the trumpets
        brayed
To joyous battle mid a storm of steeds,
Won a rich kingdom on a battle-day;
But in the sunset he was ebbing fast,
Ringed by his weeping lords. His left hand held
His white steed, to the belly plashed with blood,
That seemed to mourn him with its drooping head:
His right, his broken brand, and in his ear
His old victorious banners flapped the winds.

He called his faithful herald to his side:
"Go tell the dead I come!" With a proud smile,
The warrior with a stab let out his soul,
Which fled, and shrieked through all the other world:
"Ye dead, my master comes!" And there was pause
Till the great shade should enter.

Barbara

George Gilfillan says: "Barbara is one of the most touching little laments in the language."

ON the Sabbath-day,
    Through the churchyard old and gray,
Over the crisp and yellow leaves I held my rustling way;
And amid the words of mercy, falling on my soul like
    balms,

'Mid the gorgeous storms of music—in the mellow
    organ-calms,
'Mid the upward-streaming prayers, and the rich and
    solemn psalms,
      I stood careless, Barbara.

      My heart was otherwhere,
      While the organ shook the air,
And the priest, with outspread hands, blessed the peo-
    ple with a prayer;
But when rising to go homeward, with a mild and saint-
    like shine
Gleamed a face of airy beauty with its heavenly eyes
    on mine—
Gleamed and vanished in a moment—O that face was
    surely thine
      Out of heaven, Barbara!

      O pallid, pallid face!
      O earnest eyes of grace!
When last I saw thee, dearest, it was in another place.
You came running forth to meet me with my love-gift
    on your wrist:
The flutter of a long white dress, then all was lost in
    mist—
A purple stain of agony was on the mouth I kissed,
      That wild morning, Barbara.

      I searched, in my despair,
      Sunny noon and midnight air;
I could not drive away the thought that you were linger-
    ing there.
O many and many a winter night I sat when you were
    gone,

My worn face buried in my hands, beside the fire
    alone—
Within the dripping churchyard, the rain plashing on
    your stone,
        You were sleeping, Barbara.

      'Mong angels, do you think
      Of the precious golden link
I clasped around your happy arm while sitting by yon
    brink?
Or when that night of gliding dance, of laughter and
    guitars,
Was emptied of its music, and we watched through
    lattice-bars
The silent midnight heaven moving o'er us with its
    stars,
        Till the day broke, Barbara?

      In the years I've changed;
      Wild and far my heart has ranged,
And many sins and errors now have been on me avenged;
But to you I have been faithful whatsoever good I
    lacked:
I loved you, and above my life still hangs that love
    intact—
Your love the trembling rainbow, I the reckless cataract.
        Still I love you, Barbara.

      Yet, Love, I am unblest;
      With many doubts opprest,
I wander like the desert wind without a place of rest.
Could I but win you for an hour from off that starry
    shore,
The hunger of my soul were stilled; for Death hath told
    you more

Than the melancholy world doth know—things deeper
    than all lore
      You could teach me, Barbara.

    In vain, in vain, in vain!
      You will never come again.
There droops upon the dreary hills a mournful fringe of
    rain;
The gloaming closes slowly round, loud winds are in
    the tree,
Round selfish shores for ever moans the hurt and
    wounded sea;
There is no rest upon the earth, peace is with Death
    and thee—
      Barbara!

A Fragment from a Ballad

IN winter, when the dismal rain
    Come down in slanting lines,
And Wind, that grand old harper, smote
    His thunder harp of pines.

When violets came and woods were green,
    And larks did skyward dart,
A Love alit and white did sit
    Like an angel on his heart. . . .

The Lady Blanche was saintly fair,
    Nor proud, but meek her look:
In her hazel eyes her thoughts lay clear
    As pebbles in a brook. . . .

The world is old, oh! very old;
  The wild winds weep and rave:
The world is old, and grey, and cold,
  Let it drop into its grave.

CHRISTINA GEORGINA ROSSETTI
ENGLAND, 1830–1894

I SHARE the opinion of Edmund Clarence Stedman that Christina Rossetti, sister of Dante Gabriel Rossetti, has poetic genius of a studied and original character. She seems to me to achieve most distinction in her shorter lyrics, her longer poems being more fantastic than imaginative. At her best, she is a poet of profound and serious cast, "whose lips part with the breathing of a fervid spirit within." Her poetry is confined almost exclusively to sacred and devotional themes. Through this most rare and difficult department of the art, which so few essay without breaking up on the Scylla of doctrine on the one hand, or being whirled into the Charybdis of commonplace dullness on the other, she has steered with extraordinary success. Poetically speaking, she is the sister of George Herbert; she is of the family of Crashaw, of Vaughan, of Wither—and has affinities with Francis Thompson and Alice Meynell.

Song

WHEN I am dead, my dearest,
  Sing no sad songs for me;
Plant thou no roses at my head,
  Nor shady cypress tree:

Be the green grass above me
  With showers and dewdrops wet;

2212

And if thou wilt, remember,
  And if thou wilt, forget.

I shall not see the shadows,
  I shall not feel the rain;
I shall not hear the nightingale
  Sing on, as if in pain;

And dreaming through the twilight
  That doth not rise nor set,
Haply I may remember,
  And haply may forget.

Uphill

DOES the road wind uphill all the way?
  Yes, to the very end.
Will the day's journey take the whole long day?
  From morn to night, my friend.

But is there for the night a resting-place?
  A roof for when the slow, dark hours begin.
May not the darkness hide it from my face?
  You cannot miss that inn.

Shall I meet other wayfarers at night?
  Those who have gone before.
Then must I knock, or call when just in sight?
  They will not keep you waiting at that door.

Shall I find comfort, travel-sore and weak?
  Of labor you shall find the sum.
Will there be beds for me and all who seek?
  Yea, beds for all who come.

CHRISTINA GEORGINA ROSSETTI

Rest

O EARTH, lie heavily upon her eyes;
    Seal her sweet eyes weary of watching, Earth;
Lie close around her; leave no room for mirth
With its harsh laughter, nor for sounds of sighs.
She hath no questions, she hath no replies,
    Hushed in and curtained with a blessèd dearth
    Of all that irked her from the hour of birth;
With stillness that is almost Paradise.

Darkness more clear than noonday holdeth her,
    Silence more musical than any song;
Even her very heart has ceased to stir:
Until the morning of Eternity
Her rest shall not begin nor end, but be;
    And when she wakes she will not think it long.

Remember

REMEMBER me when I am gone away,
    Gone far away into the silent land,
When you can no more hold me by the hand
Nor I half turn to go, yet turning stay.
Remember me when no more day by day
    You tell me of our future that you planned:
    Only remember me; you understand
It will be late to counsel then or pray.

Yet if you should forget me for a while
And afterwards remember, do not grieve:
For if the darkness and corruption leave
A vestige of the thoughts that once I had,
Better by far you should forget and smile
Than that you should remember and be sad.

A Birthday

MY heart is like a singing bird
Whose nest is in a watered shoot:
My heart is like an apple-tree
Whose boughs are bent with thickset fruit:
My heart is like a rainbow shell
That paddles in a halcyon sea:
My heart is gladder than all these,
Because my love is come to me.

Raise me a dais of silk and down;
Hang it with vair and purple dyes;
Carve it in doves and pomegranates,
And peacocks with a hundred eyes;
Work it in gold and silver grapes,
In leaves, and silver fleurs-de-lys;
Because the birthday of my life
Is come, my Love is come to me.

CHRISTINA GEORGINA ROSSETTI

Roses for the Flush of Youth

OH, roses for the flush of youth,
  And laurel for the perfect prime;
But pluck an ivy branch for me
  Grown old before my time.
Oh, violets for the grave of youth,
  And bay for those dead in their prime;
Give me the withered leaves I chose
  Before in the old time.